Praise for I'm New to Government Contracting

"Get ready for an extraordinary journey into the labyrinth of government contracting with *"I'm New to Government Contracting!"* Michael's latest masterpiece is not just a book; it's a guiding light for anyone setting foot in the intricate realm of government contracting. With a rare blend of candor and wisdom, Michael shatters the misconception that the world of government contracts is a simple dichotomy. He issues a cautionary note against those who offer easy answers without delving into the complexity beneath the surface. This book is not just a manual; it's a mentor, urging you to embrace a nuanced understanding essential for navigating the intricate landscape of government contracts. In *"I'm New to Government Contracting,"* the art and science of government contracting converge, creating an indispensable compass for comprehending the subtleties of this challenging yet immensely rewarding field. Don't let this gem slip through your fingers — it's more than a book; it's your passport to success in the dynamic world of government contracting!"

Starla Halcomb, PhD, CEO, LEAD Training

"This book is incredible! It delivers a wealth of knowledge, strategies, and tactics for government contractors. Mike's insights are a beacon for companies navigating the complexities of this industry. The comprehensive approach offers not only a solid foundation but also practical advice that can be applied immediately. What sets this book apart is its ability to serve as a great starting point for companies venturing into the industry. Whether it's understanding market dynamics, implementing effective strategies, or staying ahead of the curve, Mike's instructions provide a roadmap for success.

Christa Williams, Vice President, Government Contracting Bank of America

"I recommend this book for its practical wisdom, accessibility, and relevance. Michael's real-world examples emphasize foundational principles that lay the groundwork for a solid government contracting strategy. The GovCon business isn't for the faint of heart, and he hits it head-on. Pitfalls and practical tips are sprinkled throughout, serving as invaluable tools. "Government sales is NOT about finding things to bid on. It's about finding opportunities you can WIN!" I have repeated this phrase with my seasoned BD team. Whether a novice or a seasoned entrepreneur, this book is for everyone."

Chrystal Burritt, Executive Vice President
Chickasaw Nation Industries

"This is a fantastic overview of the basics someone needs to know to enter the federal market, whether they are brand new to business or expanding their commercial business. I enjoyed reading it and picked up a few take-aways for myself. One of the best pieces of advice Mike gives is to wait on getting your 8(a) and picking a Mentor. I love that he gives such an honest opinion that is contrary to what you'll hear from most "experts.""

Christine Hopkins, CEO, ASCI

"I am blown away by this book! Easy to read yet deep and rich in content. I never underestimate the "Sage of Government Contracting," Michael LeJeune, nor should you! He has done it again. A master of business and procurement readiness, his gift for breaking down difficult and complex topics into bite sized understandable pieces places this book number one on anyone's must read list. Want to accelerate the start of your GovCon business? Start here!"

Scott Jensen, Executive Director
National Veteran Small Business Coalition

"I believe this book is a tremendous resource for new folks and established business owners, alike. The book is conversational yet informative, comprehensive yet concise... a resource I wish I had at the beginning of my small business journey! Michael LeJeune's generosity in mentorship shines through every page. This book is a must-read primer for any GovCon entrepreneur seeking to start on the right foot."

Chris Moffitt, Founder/CEO, Agile Vector, LLC

"Michael LeJeune does it again in his latest book. You learn alongside him as he shares his story of ups and downs and what ultimately made him and RSM Federal the success that it is today. Michael uses real-world examples to make the concepts easy to understand and implement. This book is like having a personal coach at your side to guide you through each step of decision making to ensure your government contracting business is able to stand out in a sea of competitors."

Tom Woodward, Chief Growth Officer, Conceras

"Government contracting can be overwhelming and confusing even for experienced business owners. Mistakes are often made by those first starting out in this space because they don't take the time to truly understand how government contracting works and more often than not, because they don't have a plan. Michael has taken a complex subject and expertly broken it down into manageable and actionable steps and strategies which, if followed, can increase your chances of success in the federal market. If you are new to GovCon, I strongly encourage you to read this book carefully from cover to cover, use it as a resource guide, and refer back as necessary!"

Shannon H. Edie, Executive Director
Native Hawaiian Organizations Association

"Michael has put together the ultimate guide for those new to government contracting (GovCon), A to Z and everything in between. From GovCon myths to you Go/No-go market entry decision; from avoiding the scam artists who promise the world then e=disappear with your money to defining your niche in terms that resonate in this market; from sub-contracting and teaming to building and managing your pipeline; RFIs, RFPs and so much more. This book needs to be in every GovCon library."

Mark Amtower, Managing Partner
Amtower & Company

"For those new to government contracting like myself, this book is a must read. It provides the ins and outs of government contracting from selecting your target market, branding, sales goals and metrics, teaming, and so much more. Take the guessing game away by following these strategies to break into government contracting."

Nia Martinez, CEO Innovative Global Learning Solutions

"This is the book I wish I'd had five years ago before I started my business, I can't imagine where we would be now if we'd had it then!"

Jeremy Casanave, CEO, Prescient Technologies

"Michael's new book has all that a growing federal contractor needs to get started on a path to success. I was especially struck by the emphasis on avoiding shortcuts. As a GovCon attorney, we sometimes hear about get-rich-quick schemes involving federal contractors. Michael puts those to bed. For instance, you have to read his takedown of the middleman strategy if you have heard about that online. Check out this book if you think you might want to get into government contracting. You won't be sorry."

Shane J. McCall, Equity Partner
Koprince McCall Pottroff LLC

"At first, I approached Michael's latest book with hesitation. Not being an avid reader, primarily due to my day being consumed by regulatory texts, I crave flare and entertainment in my rare moments of leisure reading. But to my surprise, I found myself engrossed, unable to put the book down. It shattered my expectations, proving not only informative and accurate but also highly relatable and filled with invaluable advice. Initially skeptical, I wondered if it would be just another 'fluff' book, simplifying the complexities of government business dealings. Instead, I discovered a treasure trove of wisdom, illuminating paths to avoid costly mistakes and prevent the descent into all-too-common bad habits. Furthermore, the book offered a rare glimpse into Michael's journey to becoming a revered figure in the government contracting (GovCon) sphere. This is a must-read for anyone currently in or considering entering this space. It might just be the beacon you need to navigate through the intricacies of GovCon without faltering."

Michelle Burnett, Executive Director
HUBZone Contractors National Council

"Michael helps demystify government contracting and provides the must-know information to get you started on the right foot. This book is for anyone in Government Contracting, but especially those wondering, what don't I know that I should know?"

Stephanie Marquardt, CEO, Continuous Synergy, LLC

"As always, Michael's style of delivery and content is powerful, empirical, hard-hitting, and non-sugar coated. Only read this book if you're thinking about going into GovCon, or in GovCon. It is a toolbox for succeeding in that arena. From someone that's one of that arena's most successful gladiators. Period."

Eric "Doc" Wright, PhD - Founder, Vets2PM

"I love this book!!! You knocked it out of the park, my friend. Drawing on his deep experience in the federal marketplace, Michael LeJeune has written the perfect guide for businesses looking to succeed in government sales. Packed with practical and actionable advice, and written in plain English with a touch of humor, this must-read book belongs in a prominent spot on every contractor's bookshelf."

Steven Koprince, Founder (Retired), Koprince Law

"If you are entertaining the idea of dipping your toe into Federal contracting, this book is a must read. I encourage everyone thinking about selling into the federal government to read this book before diving in head first!"

David Neal, CEO, David Neal Consulting

"This book is an easy guide for those who want to start or expand in the government contracting market. The insights are clear, actionable and practical. Anyone who follows this guide will see growth in the government market."

Jennifer Vollbrecht, President
J Vollbrecht Consulting, Inc.

"I was truly astounded by the wealth of knowledge action-packed within these pages. With over a decade of personal experience in coaching businesses, I can confidently say that Michael has left no stone unturned for contractors entering the space."

Ashley Duwel, CEO, Duwel Dev, LLC

"Michael's work here deftly integrates what people need to know in order to successfully market to Federal buyers with reminders that reinforce sales & marketing fundamentals in a way that's entirely approachable and digestible. I recommend this book to anyone who wants to shorten the learning curve for winning Federal government contracts."

Nick Bernardo, President, MyGovWatch.com

"I thoroughly enjoyed reading Michael's new book. Don't let the title fool you, this book contains valuable nuggets for experienced GovCon companies as well. The level of detailed instruction in some of the chapters would take years of trial and error to learn. The strategies and tactics in this book are vital to building the foundation of a strong and competitive GovCon business."

Travis Griffin, Vice President
Optimized Technical Solutions, Inc.

"Michael's book is an essential guide for aspiring government contractors, providing practical techniques, processes, and seasoned advice in plain English. While reading it, it appears Michael is talking to you directly, one-on-one. It's a must-read for gaining a competitive edge in the field."

Rich Earnest, Partner, Earnest Consulting Group

"Michael breaks down the otherwise complicated concepts of government contracting into bite-size chunks similar to how we operate at my organization. The step-by-step guides have had an immediate impact on my team. It has helped my team to understand the value of how to use SAM.gov and USASpending specifically."

Felisha Daemer, Vice President, Public Sector
InfusionPoints

I'm New to Government Contracting. Where Do I Start?

Learn the Exact Strategies and Tactics that Have Helped Our Clients Win Over $14.6 Billion in Government Contracts

Michael LeJeune

Copyright © 2024 by RSM Federal. All Rights Reserved.

Published by RSM Federal, Saint Louis, Missouri.

No part of this publication may be reproduced, distributed, stored in a retrieval system, or transmitted, in any form or by any means (electronic, mechanical, photocopy, recording, voice, or otherwise) without the prior written permission from the author, except in the case of very brief quotations embodied in literary reviews and certain other non-commercial uses permitted by copyright law.

Requests to the Publisher for permission should be addressed to RSM Federal, 13 Amber Wave Ct. O'Fallon, MO 63366 or contact@rsmcapitalgroup.com. Liability / Disclaimer: Although the author has used his best efforts in preparing this book, he makes no representations or warranties with respect to the accuracy or completeness of the contents of this book.

No warranty may be created or extended by sales representatives, strategic partners, affiliates, or written sales collateral. The lessons, recommendations, and strategies contained in this book may not be applicable to your specific business requirements. You should consult with a professional consultant where appropriate. The author shall not be liable for any loss of revenue or profit or incidental damages. For more information about RSM Federal, visit www.rsmfederal.com.

ISBN 979-8-9868608-1-7 (pbk)
ISBN 979-8-9868608-2-4 (ebk)

Printed in the United States of America
1 2 3 4 5 6 7 8 9 10

Other Books by RSM Federal

#1 Bestseller - The Government Sales Manual
https://www.amazon.com/dp/1733600981

#1 Bestseller - An Insider's Guide to Winning Government Contracts
https://www.amazon.com/dp/173360099X

#1 Bestseller - Game Changers for Government Contractors
https://www.amazon.com/dp/1733600949

#1 Bestseller – Becoming a GovCon Expert
https://www.amazon.com/dp/1733600965

Contents

Praise for I'm New to Government Contracting i

Contents xi

Foreword 15

Special Thanks 17

Federal Access Resources 18

Introduction 19

Chapter 1. How I Became a Government Contractor 23

Chapter 2. Myth-Busting and Lessons Learned 35

Chapter 3. Why the Middleman Strategy is a Scam 45

Chapter 4. Identifying and Avoiding Con Artists 51

Chapter 5. Is Government Contracting Right For You? 55

Chapter 6. Procurement Readiness 71

Chapter 7. Picking Your Niche 79

Chapter 8. Branding Yourself and Your Company 83

Chapter 9. Social Media Strategy Considerations 89

Chapter 10. Intro to Value-Mapping™ 95

Chapter 11. Nine Core Marketing Tools 101

Chapter 12. Seven Key Elements of a Great Capability Statement ... 107

Chapter 13. Sales Goals and Metrics 111

Chapter 14. Seven Key Ways to Build Your Pipeline 117

Chapter 15. Managing Your Pipeline 123

Chapter 16. Six Ways to Reach Contracting Officers 131

Chapter 17. Capability Briefings 135

Chapter 18. Seven Tips for Writing Better Emails 139

Chapter 19. Teaming With Other Companies 143

Chapter 20. Eight Ways Primes Evaluate Subcontractors 149

Chapter 21. RFIs and Sources Sought 155

Chapter 22. The RFP Process 159

Chapter 23. SAP and Micro Purchases 171

Chapter 24. Introduction to Contract Vehicles 175

Chapter 25. Preparing to Kick Off a New Contract 183

Chapter 26. Mentor Protege 187

Chapter 27. Key Hires Along the Way 191

Chapter 28. Conferences 195

Chapter 29. FAR References 201

Chapter 30. The Marathon Mindset 205

Chapter 31. Hiring a Coach 213

A Small Favor 219

Other RSM Federal Resources 220

About RSM Federal 222

About Michael LeJeune 223

Acronyms 225

Foreword

Edward Spenceley
National Government Contracting Executive
Bank of America

The title of this book, "I'm new to government contracting. Where do I start?" asks a question that I hear over and over again by companies and business professionals that want to win government contracts. The answer is easier than you think...*you start at the beginning*. The beginning is by reading this book. You have heard the phrase, "work smarter not harder," but the reality is that you need to work smarter and harder. You control how hard you work at something. This book gives you the smarter part of the equation.

I have had hundreds of people ask me "where do I start?" and then these same professionals try answering their own question before I can even respond! As if by talking through it they can convince themselves, and me, what it should look like and how it should be done. If you really want to know "the what and the how," the chapters in this book provide the steps you need to take. Michael's step-by-step concepts are plainly, candidly, and methodically spelled-out. More important, Michael has written in a tone of voice, with simple concepts, that will appeal to any reader.

Understanding the "why," dictates the "what and how." For me "the why" is literally the mission of our Armed Services and the federal agencies. My role today, as the senior executive at Bank of America for government programs, is not much different from when I was a team leader and senior non-commissioned officer (NCOIC) in the U.S. Army. I do what I do today to support the end user; the Soldier, Sailor, Marine, Airman, the agency intelligence asset, the special operator, and those deployed down-range. I do this today through industry.

Michael allows industry to live their why, by showing them the what and the how; the steps you need to take; the pitfalls you need to avoid; and how to make your why a reality.

I recognize the impact that Michael has on the government contracting community. The information he shares in this book provides a roadmap that, frankly, will accelerate your success. Michael's expertise is well respected in the government market. Don't simply take my word for it. I constantly hear about Michael, time and time again, from industry partners, clients (RSM Federal's and Bank of America's), and government accountants and attorneys. You only have to attend a National conference and walk by RSM Federal's booth to see how many people want to talk to Michael.

Michael LeJeune is a bestselling author, master coach with RSM Federal, and a one-man accelerator for those brave enough to take the path less traveled through government contracting. His podcast, Game Changers for Government Contractors, with more than 440,000 downloads, is a testament to the fundamental truths outlined in this book. I manage the government team at Bank of America. This book and all the other resources in RSM Federal's ecosystem are a great resource for me, my team, and our clients.

Two years ago, we were at the National 8a Small Business Conference in New Orleans. My team was nominated for Vendor Partner of the Year. We were grateful for the nomination and recognition as one of the top banks supporting government contractors. We placed second to Michael LeJeune and Joshua Frank, the dynamic duo that runs RSM Federal. I chuckle when I say, "we didn't protest the results of the award" (like companies often do when they lose a contract.) Instead, *we engaged and celebrated their success*; recognizing that Michael and the RSM Federal team were professionals we wanted to work with, to team with in the future!

Their passion, their why, is aligned with ours.

Enjoy the read and enjoy the journey. In the future, when someone asks you the question, "where do I start?" tell them to take a breath and hand them this book.

> Edward Spenceley
> National Government Contracting Executive
> Senior Vice President
> Bank of America

Special Thanks

I want to personally thank my friend and business partner Joshua Frank for two things. First, Josh edits all of my books, creates graphics for me, and manages the process on the backend with Amazon. It's a lot of work and I couldn't get these books to market without his help.

Second, Josh and I have known each other for over twenty years. We've been co-workers, friends, and business partners in that time. It was ultimately Josh that lured me back into the government market after multiple years in the commercial market. Over the last decade working together, I've learned a lot of what I know today about government contracting from Josh. I've picked his brain on almost a daily basis. In fact, I still pick his brain on a very regular basis. I affectionately refer to him as Rain Man because of his extensive knowledge of the government.

With that in mind, it would be a disservice to Josh if I didn't give him credit for many of the ideas, concepts, and strategies that I discuss in this book. For example, Josh coined the phrases "value-mapping" and "ghosting." He's also turned the market upside down by focusing on strategies like: not using your status upfront, but as a balancing differentiator and teaching people how to use metrics (through value-mapping) to demonstrate value and past performance. I may have written the words in this book, but it's very much a collaborative effort between the two of us.

Federal Access Resources

It's impossible for me to cover everything you need in a single book. Whenever possible, I will reference a template, video, or some other resource in Federal Access (FA) and I will use the logo below to bring this to your attention.

 Federal Access is our coaching and training platform for government contractors. At the time of writing this book, we have more than 200 strategy guides, 100+ templates, a webinar archive, more than 150 training playbooks, email SME support, and weekly live sessions (Inner Circle) with myself, Josh, and other industry experts. It's a tremendous value for members and a bargain for the support you get. I highly recommend that you check it out if you aren't already a member.

While I'm writing this, we are in the middle of supercharging the Federal Access platform. Just be aware that the location for some of the files, videos, and other resources in Federal Access are likely to change over the next several months.

Use this link: https://Federal-access.com/NewToGovConBook to get 20% off your membership.

Introduction

The advice I'm going to give you in this book applies to 95% of you. This is the path that almost every government contractor is going to take. Are there exceptions? Absolutely! But only about 5% will be the exception. Maybe less. The average government contractor takes three to five years of stumbling through this market before they win even a single contract. Some never win a contract and eventually either go out of business, flip over to the commercial market, or get a job. The reason so many people fail is that everyone thinks they are in the 5% and don't have to follow the process. That's just not true.

Over the last 20 years of being a coach, I've conducted thousands of coaching sessions and consultations. What have I learned during that time? The process that I'm going to share with you in this book WORKS! It requires persistence, but it works. For example, you aren't likely to win a contract after just a single capability briefing with a contracting officer. But you will if you persist! It's just a matter of time and working the system.

My favorite answer isn't maybe, but I do use it a lot. The truth is that a lot of questions are not black and white. There are quite a few nuances to every situation. Even the simplest question could result in a maybe based on what your company does, your size, status, target agency, ownership, new rule changes, and other factors. Besides giving you a heads up to this, my secondary point is that you should be weary of anyone who gives you direct answers with no context. Those people are typically called con artists.

It's important to note that the majority of my experience is with Federal contracting. A lot of the tactics and strategies you will learn are market agnostic, but they were written with the Federal market in mind and not the SLED market.

Don't know what the SLED market is? You're not alone. The government is littered with acronyms. I've included an acronym list at the back of the book for your reference.

Another thing you will notice is that I focus a lot on service based businesses. Again, the tactics and strategies are agnostic, but I work almost exclusively with service-based companies. There are other members of my team that work heavily in the product arena.

I'll also note that if you are a product-based company, you almost certainly need to know about DLA and DIBBS. I don't cover that topic in this book in detail, but we have an entire section in Federal Access that covers DLA and DIBBS.

Everything you learn in this book is one more tool, tip, or trick that goes in your tool bag as a business owner. Initially, you may only have a screwdriver and a hammer in your bag of tricks. The goal of this book is to help fill up your tool bag and help you understand some of the nuances of when and where to use each tool. That is where the *Art and Science of Government Sales*™ collide.

I know that a lot of people will skip around in this book. For that reason, I cover some topics multiple times throughout the book. I tried to connect the dots anywhere that they are key so that you don't miss any nuances by skipping around in the book. This also serves as a constant reminder for key points.

The Values That Shape My Life

Someone can be a great coach and not be a good fit for you. I'm a simple farm boy from Louisiana. You will likely see me in a ball cap, jeans, and a hoodie 95% of the time. If it's warm, I'm in shorts. I consider warm anything above 50 degrees. I don't have a big family. My parents have passed. So, my clients are my adopted family. I love and care about all of them. This isn't just a business for me. It's my passion and its personal.

I consider myself a Christian, but can't stand religion. Over the years, I've been involved in church groups. I've spoken on stage in churches. I've even run my own home church when nothing else seemed to fit our family. But...I can't stand religion.

I believe business should be fun. I think your business should serve you and not the other way around. If done properly, your business should spit out a ton of cash that allows you to live your wildest dreams. My purpose on this planet is to inspire other to chase their dreams.

I believe in treating people with respect while also being truthful. You don't have to be a jerk to share the truth with someone.

I believe you can't pay me enough to work with some people. I don't have the time or energy to devote myself to negative situations. On that same note, you can't pay me enough to compromise my values. There isn't a contract, client, or deal big enough to change who I am as a person.

That's a glimpse of my values. I'm unapologetic about them. I'm not for everyone. I get that. I may not be for you. That's cool. I don't hold that against you. :)

The takeaway is that you should only work with someone that aligns with your values. Does it have to be 100%? Nope. Joshua Frank and I don't agree on everything. But we share the same core values.

Before you go any further, I have a quick recommendation. Connect with me on LinkedIn if we are not already connected. Here's the direct link to my profile: https://www.linkedin.com/in/michaeljlejeune/

You will be hard pressed to find anyone on LinkedIn who puts out more content, coverage, and engages in government market discussions more than I do. Connecting with me guarantees that you will continue learning and growing in this market. It also means you have a direct line to me if you ever need anything.

As always, I'm here to help.

Michael LeJeune

Chapter 1.
How I Became a Government Contractor

I'm going to walk you through exactly how I got started in government contracting. I'm going back to the beginning to give you some context because I think it's really important for you to hear how a kid in his early 20's, who had never had any sales training, business training, or government contractor training got into the market and then built a team that won millions in government contracts.

If I can do this, anybody can do it. I'm not saying it's easy. I'm saying it's possible. That's the takeaway. I'm saying it's possible. I really feel like the story is incomplete if I just start from when I took over our sales department and started leading it and the things we did. That's not where the story really begins.

You will learn how I got into the market, how and why I joined the sales team, and most important, how we were able to grow from a struggling company to north of $11 million annually in less than two years.

My backstory serves a couple of purposes. The first one is that is shows how little I understood this market. The second is that it gives insight to the type of person I am. I'm not a quitter. Even though I'm not a Marine, I embody their motto of Improvise, Adapt, and Overcome. You will see that over the course of the next few pages.

The story begins with me in the Army. I joined the Army in 1995. I was in from 1995 to 1999, all of that time at Fort Hood in the Force XXI program. The Force XXI program was very interesting because we were focused on next generation tools, technologies, software, vehicles, and aircraft for the government.

I was constantly surrounded by government contractors. Lockheed Martin, General Dynamics, MITRE, SAIC, you name the company, and they were there. They were embedded with us all the time to get feedback on their technology and to make changes on the fly.

What happens when you're a young soldier and you see Defense contractors around you all the time? You start asking questions about how they became a government contractor and what that process looks like. I asked questions about how they got their job, the kind of money they were making, and how I could follow in their footsteps.

Then there's this natural progression where you see your fellow soldiers getting out of the military and getting a coveted contractor job. Nature takes its course and you start positioning yourself (at least I did) for one of those contractor jobs.

When I got out of the military, I contacted the colonel that I had worked for in the military. He was with GTE at the time. I asked if he had any spots open on his team and just like that, I became a government contractor. Next thing I know, I was moving to Colorado Springs and I was working on GTE's help desk.

I didn't have my degree at the time, but I knew the boss. That's when I first learned how powerful relationships were going to be to my future. I didn't technically meet the requirements, but it was more about who I knew than anything else. After all, my colonel knew my capabilities from working side-by-side with me for nearly three years.

The help desk was right up my alley. I loved problem solving, but I was scared to death of talking to strangers on the phone. But I increased my salary by about 500% and that helped with my shyness.

I was trained on one of the first collaborative software tools for the government. I learned how to troubleshoot the software, how to install it, work on the servers, and train users. Training was about two weeks and then we were thrown to the wolves on the help desk. My goal when I joined that team was to be running the help desk in five years. I thought that would make me king of the mountain.

Flash forward two years and I'm the Director of Sales. I had spent those two years working every single day with our government contracting clients. I was working with military and civilians, program managers, contracting officers, and hundreds of users. The best part was working with all of the agencies and not only understanding how they used our software, how they purchased it, and most important, WHO was purchasing it. I had the pleasure of working with the intelligence community, Joint Forces Commands, the Army, Navy, Air Force, and more.

I was working with them on a daily basis. They were calling me. We were on a first name basis. And I was getting to know all of these people. That was one of the things that made me successful in sales. I got to know every single customer by name.

I Join the Dark Side

How did I wind up on the sales team in the first place? I was the supervisor of the help desk, and I get an offer from another company to leave. It was a $5,000 raise. I brought that offer to my supervisor and he laughed at me. He didn't skip a beat. He said he wasn't interested in matching the offer and I should just take it and leave. He wouldn't even discuss it with me.

The first thing I did before accepting the other offer was to call my colonel friend. He was my vice president at the time. I gave him the heads up that I was getting ready to leave. It was a similar situation as the Army. I couldn't get a raise and there was no room for a promotion. I was stuck in this position.

The colonel asked me if I would consider a position on the sales team instead of leaving? I initially said no. That's literally the dark side of the company. There's absolutely no reason for me to go over to the dark side. Then he says, "this move will triple your compensation." The next thing out of my mouth was, "tell me about the dark side!"

As you already know, I took the job in sales. Immediately, I started having success and it totally dumbfounded my new boss. He couldn't understand how I was closing sales in my first quarter. They didn't expect anything out of me for six months.

What was the difference between me and the other sales guys? Relationships! I had been building relationships with our entire client base for two years. They knew me by first name. They knew little things about me. I knew little things about them like their favorite pastime, sports teams, hobbies, etc. The most important thing they knew about me was that I delivered on my promises. In fact, I usually overdelivered. This meant that I had earned their trust. Did I mention, it took two years? Yes, but I wanted to remind you.

When I was assigned my client list, I started reaching out and talking to them. I already knew their problems. That made me less of a "salesperson" and more of a trusted problem solver. I can't stress how important it is for you to know the customer and understand their problems. I knew the things they had been complaining about since day one on the help desk. The difference is that now I was in a position to fix their problems without layers of management telling me no.

Once we started fixing things that were high priority for the clients, the clients had an epiphany. They realized that I actually cared about what was important to them. They in turn decided to start buying more software. They started buying more licenses and expanding the usage of the tool. And immediately I started getting sales where other sales people were not because *they did not understand the clients*.

Some of our sales people were what I consider old school sales. They were the kind of folks that wanted to take prospects out to dinner or for a round of golf. They didn't understand that you can't do this in government sales. Not only is it against the regulations, it doesn't mean the prospect is going to buy from you.

About eight months go by and I'm just crushing it in sales. I knew at the time the company as a whole was struggling. Our department had been sold off to General Dynamics and then again to a very small company. We went from being part of a multi-billion-dollar company to a company with less than $50 million in revenue that was on a sharp decline.

The reason this small company bought our software was because this was going to be their silver bullet that allowed them to enter the government market and save the day. In reality, the leadership had no clue on how to build a business in the government market and almost zero patience with our sales team. They didn't understand how long it takes to do anything in the government. Promises had been made by the seller and those promises weren't coming to fruition.

I was called into a last-minute meeting one day. I'd just sold my house in Colorado and I was moving to the St. Louis area. This meeting was supposed to be about who was buying us or who was going to inject some cash into the company to keep us going long enough to build the government business.

I had a new VP of sales by this time and he called me before the meeting. It was a heads up that I needed to be on the call. There was "super exciting news." He said that someone was injecting $20 million in cash and it was going to be awesome!

I get in the meeting and as you can imagine, it doesn't go the way you expect. In the meeting, the CEO says, "There were three companies that looked like they were going to put money into the company, but all three have backed out."

This is where we expect the CEO to say there's going to be a fourth company or some other miracle. Instead, the CEO says that everything has failed and as of this moment, you're all fired. Yep. The entire company was let go.

I remember hanging up on that meeting and thinking that I was about to go into the mortgage company and sell my house, move across the country, and I had just lost my job. My heart sank.

My wife and I were staying in a hotel that morning because we had already packed up our house and sent all of our belongings with movers half way across the country. There was no turning back. We went to closing and acted like nothing had happened.

After closing, my wife asked the million-dollar question, "what do we do now?" I simply said that we were going to get in the cars and head to the new house. I figured we would come up with a plan between Colorado and St. Louis.

Sure enough, about halfway through my drive, I get a call from my old boss. "We want you back…but there's a catch. We need you to take a 20% pay cut." What was I supposed to do? I had to take it. We had a new house to pay for.

An hour later, my boss calls me back and says, "Change of plans. We still want you back. No pay cut!" Now I was actually excited to be making the exact amount I was making before I was fired. I would later find out this was all a slick plan to make this guy look like a savior.

The next day, I was asked to sit in on yet another CEO meeting. I was told that they loved me because I was the only guy hitting his numbers. While that was true, the CEO didn't show any love for anyone on the call. It was a solid hour of yelling at us for how much we sucked, which led to the biggest risk of my career. I stepped-up in that moment and challenged him on everything he was telling us.

At some point he cut me off and stopped the meeting. The next phone call was directly from the CEO. He said my story didn't match up with what he knew was going on. He was confused why our stories were so different. The short version is that our boss had been lying to everyone. To the CEO, the salespeople, and everyone else about the current state of affairs.

I Take Over the Sales Team

After about 30 minutes of my side of the story, the CEO says, "Just so you know, your boss is my next call and he's getting fired. Who should replace him?" I was 26 at the time, didn't have any formal sales training, and barely knew anything about government contracting or leading a sales team. And yet, I said the only thing I could think of, "the only person I trust to run the sales team is me."

The next thing out of the CEO's mouth was, "Good. You're the new director of sales. Take the weekend to think through your strategy. I'll see you in DC in your new office."

I didn't even know what a sales strategy was and now I have to come up with one over the weekend, for a publicly traded company! I knew this was going to be rough. This is how I would kick off a two-year commute from St. Louis to Washington D.C.

I flew into Washington the following Monday and was introduced to the sales team as their new director. The team was still happy to have a job. They didn't think much of the young punk that had just been named their boss. My first act as sales director was to ask everyone to see their pipeline. You've never seen so many blank stares in your life. No one had a pipeline or anything resembling a pipeline. That's the first moment that I thought I might fail in this role.

Our First Sales Pipeline

Within the first two weeks, we had the first sales pipeline in the company. We started simple. I gathered everyone in the conference room and we built the pipeline together. Initially, we threw everything into one spreadsheet and ranked it by percentage. That allowed me to weight the pipeline and determine if we had enough opportunities to meet our quarterly goals. We didn't, but that was okay. We were finally organized and on our way.

When I took over the team, we had 13 folks on the sales team. Only a couple of them were hitting their numbers. They didn't have clear metrics, so the next thing I did was implement quarterly sales goals and monthly metrics to help identify what was actually going on with my team.

They didn't like it.

The metrics showed that people were more interested in golf than doing sales. I quickly took our sales team from 13 down to two. Yes, from 13 to two in about two months. Then I hired two additional folks. One of which is my business partner Joshua Frank, for a total of 4 of us on the team.

The next thing that I started working on was a long-term pipeline. Our "pipeline" had four major buckets based on percentage, instead of stages, and the focus was about what was going to close THIS quarter. The buckets were: 25%, 50%, 75%, and 100%. I know what you're thinking. This is really creative. All joking aside, this was a massive innovation in a situation where the alternative was no tracking at all.

Over the course of six months, I began to refine the pipeline with notes and I built it twelve months out. This gave us a clear picture for the first time in the company about what to expect for an entire year. I also began to get very good at judging what was going to close each month and I used this as a tool to determine what the next steps or touch points were for each opportunity. This simple pipeline was a game changer for us.

An unexpected benefit of having a pipeline was that the confidence of our CEO and board of director's grew around our team. Before the pipeline, there was a lot of tension and pressure on the entire team because no one had a clue what to expect. As I got better at predicting revenue, all of those fears and concerns melted away. They could look at the pipeline and with confidence know what our team was going to close that quarter.

The final benefit of having a pipeline was that it allowed me to clearly measure team performance. I was able to quickly tell who had enough opportunities in their portion of the pipeline and who wasn't going to make their numbers. This allowed me to predict where to invest my time with the team and with potential customers. In the past, the company would wait until the end of the year to evaluate how much commission they had paid out and waited to take corrective action. Usually by firing someone. The old way wasn't a good model for the team or the company and it needed to change.

The pipeline allowed us to monitor the team on a monthly basis and to provide coaching and assistance throughout the year. This led to me having to fire one employee because they weren't making their numbers for several months in a row and weren't putting in the necessary work to get there. Instead of waiting a year, this happened much faster and allowed us to replace this person with a more productive salesperson in a fraction of the time it would have normally taken.

Shifting Our Business Model

My next big change was evaluating our business model. One of the things that I noticed was that we were selling through resellers. We didn't sell direct. Everything we sold was through value-added resellers or VARs. What I noticed was that the VA was missing in VAR.

There was no value add to the customer. I sat down with the CEO and I said, "Our margin is garbage right now. We're making 20% margin on these licenses at best. Sometimes, we're making 15%. We're selling indirect to our customers. Where there should be value add, there's zero value add. To make matters worse, we are doing all the sales work and these "VARs" are making more money than us. This madness has to stop!"

With all that in mind, we decided to end our VAR program. We decided to sell direct to the government. By changing our business model, we were able to decrease the cost of the licenses and quadruple our profit.

Now that we were making more profit, I was able to reduce the cost to the customer and exponentially increase profitability. Did everyone love the idea? Absolutely not! In fact, I made a LOT of people mad. I remember sitting in one of the towers in Tyson's Corner with General Dynamics. It was a bit intimidating. It seemed like the 800th floor of the building. One of their VPs sat across from me and said, "This is BS and you know it. I've been in this business 40 years and you don't do this kind of thing." I just remember looking back at him and saying, "You're running a $3 billion division of GD and we are a $3-million-dollar company struggling to survive. What's BS is you taking 80% off the top of OUR PRODUCT!"

Remember, I was in my mid-twenties at the time. The look on his face was priceless. I think I had that happen to me a few times with some of our big partners. They weren't happy about it, but I did two things to ease the pain. I let them know they could have the services on the backend. We didn't want any of that work. I also gave them six months for transition.

In the first three to five months, I received a lot of pushback; a lot of hate. But as time went on, we began to mend relationships. The other great thing that happened is that we started to hit our tipping point. That meant increased license sales. We went from around a thousand licenses a year to 10,000 licenses a year. And guess what that meant? A lot more work on the back end for our partners. As their revenues grew, they seemed to forget about our change to the model.

Becoming Lean and Mean

The next item on my agenda was to see if I could reduce other costs. Part of our software was built on this other company's software, so we had to license it in addition to licensing our portion of the product. As a surprise to us, that company sold to Microsoft. When that company got sold to Microsoft, we were told there wouldn't be any negotiating on price. So, what did I do? I flew out to Redmond and I met with the team at Microsoft and I humbly asked for their help.

Initially, they wouldn't budge so I gambled. I offered to guarantee that if they would help us on pricing, we would see a 10X growth in the business. And what did they say? After they finished laughing, they said yes! If you guarantee revenue, we'll absolutely lower your costs. They wound up giving us almost 50% off the current price. This allowed us to be very profitable in the government market.

At this point, we began to hit our stride and it was all about hard work. We started working on the relationships I had built. I started teaching our sales people how to build these relationships as well. What questions to ask to see if their customers had the same problems my customers had. And guess what happened? All of their accounts started growing. Everybody started selling a lot more. As we started to sell more, one of the really cool things that happened was the government started coming to us to buy licenses in bulk. This allowed us to go back to Microsoft to negotiate new rates for bulk/volume pricing.

How I Wound Up on the FBI's Watch List

As we approached the end of my first year as sales director, we broke the $4M mark in sales. Our greatest year prior to this was roughly $1.2M. Instead of being complacent, I asked the team for ideas to take things to the next level. Someone on the team suggested the wildest thing I'd ever heard. They suggested that we create an unsolicited proposal and send it to everyone in the government. And so we did!

We built a 200-page PowerPoint presentation, printed it, and put it in binders. We spent several late nights assembling binders and addressing them by hand. We started to mail them to every secretary, undersecretary, and anyone else with a significant title in the military. Then we started hitting the joint commands and intel agencies with the same packet. We somehow found President George Bush's fax number for his war room and his private email address. I jokingly tell people that I'm sure I'm still on an FBI watch list somewhere for this stunt.

We started emailing and faxing. Yes, faxing this 200 and something page unsolicited proposal to everybody under the sun. We were so cool. We thought it was amazing. It felt a bit like a Jerry McGuire moment. Those late nights were filled with energy and excitement.

What was the result? Crickets! Months and months of crickets. Finally, about month four, I receive a signed letter from Andy Card, President Bush's Chief of Staff. The gist of the letter was that while they appreciated what we were trying to accomplish, the President wasn't the person I needed to talk to. Reading the letter, I started to feel crushed. Then, at the bottom of the letter, was a glimmer of hope. Mr. Card gave me a name. He told me I needed to speak to a specific three-star general.

Now that I was armed with a signed letter from the President's chief of staff, I was off and running again. I started using that letter to open doors. While we didn't get the blanket license deal that I was hoping for, we did open a lot of doors that I never thought would've opened. All of a sudden, there were people that knew about us. There were people that were reaching out to ask questions. All of a sudden, our pipeline went from about 15 contract opportunities a quarter up to about 40.

Everything accelerated from this point on. We kept proactively talking to our customers and positioning our solution. Customers responded and we ended my second year as the sales director just north of $11M in sales.

Documenting What We Learned

Josh did a way better job than I did of documenting our lessons learned in the moment and he eventually released The Government Sales Manual based largely on these lessons learned at this company and his role at other government firms. The manual has been refined over the years and is currently in its 10th edition at the time of writing this. You can get a copy of The Government Sales Manual on Amazon here: https://www.amazon.com/dp/1733600981

If you join any level of Federal Access, you also get a searchable PDF version of the manual.

While Josh had the foresight to document all of our learnings in the moment, I did not. It took me over 20 years of working in the market to finally document the exact process that we used. That's what the rest of this book is about. It outlines everything you need to do so you don't waste time getting up to speed in this market.

The good news is that while these are the same basic steps we used back then, everything has been updated, tested, and refined during the last 20 years. In fact, our clients have been using these tactics and strategies since 2008. As a result, our clients have won over $14.6 billion in direct government contracts and over $30 billion in IDIQs.

Does that mean you are going to win a billion dollars or even a million dollars by reading this book? Our lawyers need me to make it clear that you might not win a single contract or earn a single dollar by reading this book.

Here's my promise to you. If you read through the whole book, take notes, and actually apply what you've learned, you are going to gain some benefit. How much is up to you.

Chapter 2.
Myth-Busting and Lessons Learned

The next few pages may feel a bit like I'm hopping on a soapbox on a few issues, but stick with me. There's some really important stuff in here. I want you to know the truth about some of the biggest myths and lessons learned that our clients have had over the years. And yes, some of these are a soapbox for me. I want you to avoid these common mistakes so you can start winning contracts faster than the average government contractor.

I need to ask a favor of you before you go any further in the book. I want you to read this chapter for what it is. It's easy to read the next few pages and get discouraged because you either believe one of these myths or you made one or more of these mistakes. That's all right. In fact, consider it a good thing if you've gotten some of these mistakes out of the way.

You can also look at this chapter as being full of ah-ha moments. Many of our most successful clients have made most or all of these mistakes. Some of them multiple times. In fact, many clients are in what I call a mistake loop because they don't know that what they are doing is either incorrect, not a best practice, or just a myth. How can you be expected to break out of a mistake loop if you don't know you are in it? That's unrealistic.

You will likely find yourself saying, "that's why this isn't working," over and over again. That's an ah-ha moment. Those moments should encourage you because now that you know what you are doing wrong, you can change your approach and start seeing results. Enjoy the next few pages of ah-ha moments.

A status is not a golden ticket. Getting a status won't initially be a game changer for you. Think about it for a minute. If you are competing on a small business, WOSB, 8(a), or SDVOSB contract; what's the one thing you have in common with everyone else competing for that contract? If you answered your status, you're correct! In this situation, your status gives you the ability to compete. You will ultimately win or lose the contract based on how well you communicate your value and how you price your product and services. Your status is one tool in your tool bag and it's not a sledgehammer.

Your status does not exempt you from the core fundamentals. Yep! I hate to break it to you, but you still need to be able to tell a great story in your corporate overview. You need to put together an awesome capability statement. You have to get some of your past performance the hard way through teaming. You need to learn the rules in the Federal Acquisition Regulation (FAR) for your status. You will find that sole source contracts are elusive. Finally, you need a solid business strategy.

In most cases, your status should NOT be the first thing you tell someone about your company. "Your value is not your status." ~ *Joshua Frank*. The companies that open their pitch with, "We are an 8(a), WOSB, SDVOSB, etc." come off as immature to the government and teaming partners. If you say those words to a contracting officer, they will either roll their eyes, die a little inside, or both.

I guarantee you that you are going to come across a "mentor" that tells you to plaster your status all over every piece of marketing material you have and for that to be the first thing that comes out of your mouth when you introduce your company.

They are wrong.

There are a few rare cases where I would advise you to have your status near the beginning of your pitch, but those cases are very rare. For example, if you are meeting with an Office of Small & Disadvantaged Business Utilization (OSDBU), your status should come up early in the conversation. But I still wouldn't lead with it. I would open with your value.

Do NOT get your 8(a) out of the gate before you have a solid strategy. This single piece of advice could help you make millions. I can't tell you how many 8(a) companies I've talked to that are in year five or later and haven't figured out how to take advantage of their 8(a) status or how to win a contract. They rushed out and got the status when they were new to the market. They didn't have any government clients yet. Worst of all, they didn't have a plan. They thought their 8(a) was a golden ticket and ultimately beat their head against a wall for years. Don't be one of those companies. Wait, put together a solid market strategy, and develop relationships with your top agencies and teaming partners! I would also advise you to get some past performance. Win three to five contracts. THEN get your 8(a).

"But Mike, what if I made the mistake and got my 8(a) early?" I'm glad you asked. LOL! Do exactly what I said in the last paragraph. No matter how you try to avoid it, your 8(a) will come to an end. It is what it is. All you can do is your best to put your company on track to land a few 8(a) contracts before you graduate. But guess what? It's not the end of the world if you don't take advantage of it. With or without your status, you still need a plan. You still need relationships. You still need past performance. Work the fundamentals and you will grow your business well beyond your 8(a) graduation.

Don't try to get a Mentor Protégé relationship out of the gate. The average person wouldn't walk up to someone on a busy street and ask them to get married. And yet, this happens constantly in government contracting. You meet a company at an event and the next thing you know; you're talking about a mentor protégé relationship.

If getting a mentor protégé relationship is something on your roadmap, my advice is to talk to a few companies before going down this road. Interview them over a couple of meetings before you consider getting serious. Once you realize you actually like the other company, ask them to team on a contract or two. Work together to see if the company is simply on their best behavior during the dating period.

Teaming with another company allows you to peek under the hood of their operations. You get a better feel for how they approach an RFP. Win or lose, you will get to see how they handle winning and losing. Will they forget about you if they lose? Will they give you work or forget about you when they win? What's their quality of work? Do clients like them? Do they have a solid reputation in the market with other contractors? Do they have influence/relationships in the market? Are they willing to mentor you during the teaming process? *Do they pay your invoices on time?* You only find out this stuff from working together.

I discuss Mentor Protégé relationships more in-depth in Chapter 26.

Don't talk to a teaming partner until you've done your research. A common challenge that I hear from contractors is that they can't get a prime to call them back. They reached out to the prime because they are a small business and they were hoping to leverage their status to win a subcontract.

The meeting went something like this. "Hi Prime, we are a small WOSB/8(a). We would like to team with you if you have any cyber security contracts in the near future."

The prime will typically respond with something like this. "Thank you for reaching out. It sounds like you are very good at what you do. Please send us your capability statement and if something pops up in the future, we will give you a call."

You walk away from a meeting like this super excited. Then you wait and nothing happens. You never get that call because you wind up in a stack of capability statements with hundreds of other companies.

The reason this is happening to you is because you didn't do your homework. You came-in unprepared.

I discuss teaming a lot in this book. Chapters 19 and 20 are devoted to this topic.

You probably don't need a GSA Schedule. Would it shock you to know that we typically only recommend a GSA Schedule to about 15% of our clients? People tend to look at a GSA Schedule similar to their status. They think it's a golden ticket.

Here are some numbers for you. I pulled these directly out of the GSA Sales Query Tool. The report I viewed covered all GSA Schedules that were awarded from FY1995 to FY2022 (28 years).

- 55,037   GSA Schedules awarded
- 28,040   terminated
- 13,664   expired
- 12,775   are currently active

- 50.39%   did not meet the min sales in years 1 &2.
- 52.06%   did not meet the min sales in year 3.
- 47.07%   did not meet the min sales in year 4.
- 40.91%   did not meet the min sales in year 5.

If GSA Schedules are a golden ticket, then why do 50% of all schedule holders never win a contract via GSA and ultimately lose their schedule? The simple answer is because *it's not a golden ticket*. The data backs this up.

The belief is that thousands of government buyers are using GSA Schedules like Amazon buyers, that they are spending hours every day scouring GSA Schedules just looking for ways to spend their contract dollars. That's simply not true. At least, it's not the norm.

GSA is a vehicle to get the job done for a contracting officer. It's part of the acquisition strategy. But, it's not the only vehicle that they have at their fingertips. It's just one of many acquisition options.

Having a GSA Schedule does not exclude you from needing to do the same business development activities as you did before you were awarded your GSA Schedule. You have to meet with buyers, respond to RFIs, and market your business.

Contract vehicles in general. Similar to GSA, companies tend to have a general belief that they need the latest and greatest contract vehicle. The problem with this is that you need to verify direction before going down this road. It doesn't matter how popular OASIS, STARS III, or some other vehicle is. You need to verify that your target agencies are using that contract vehicle. Otherwise, you are wasting your time. More on contract vehicles in chapter 24.

Do you really know who your client is? Everyone thinks they know who buys what they sell. But most don't and they waste years pursuing the wrong prospects. A few years ago, a client came to me and told me that they needed help getting into the Department of Transportation. They had wasted three years trying to break into the department with literally zero results. They also told me that while they could work nationwide, they wanted to avoid Texas because they didn't have an office there.

I did about twenty minutes of research and discovered two things. The first is that the top buyer for what they sell was the Department of Defense. Specifically, the Army Corp of Engineers. The second thing I discovered was that over 60% of the work they were looking for was in Texas. When I looked at the number, DOT wasn't even on the radar. Out of the billions spent under their North American Industrial Classification Code (NAICS), only about $100K was procured by DOT in the last 10 years.

This client, like many others, was chasing the wrong rabbit! Now, it all made sense why no one wanted to speak to them. It only takes a little research on a few free websites to determine if your assumptions are correct.

Just hunt for opportunities in SAM. 80% of opportunities aren't in the System for Award Management (SAM), YET! Have you ever heard someone say, "that opportunity is wired for company ABC?" That's because most opportunities go through a lengthy pre-acquisition process BEFORE they wind up on SAM. During that process, companies will ghost their capabilities and work their relationships at an agency to get their requirements into an RFP.

I will go into more detail on ghosting in chapter 21 where I describe how ghosting communicates your strengths and highlights your competitor's weaknesses.

You need to be spending your time building relationships and working more on pre-acquisition efforts as opposed to just responding to opportunities in SAM. Most companies have this backwards and tend to only respond to things that are already deep into the acquisition process.

Have you ever heard the phrase, "If the first time you heard about an opportunity is when you saw it on SAM, you've already lost?" Most companies have heard of this and yet, they still don't fix their strategy. I believe the reason for this is very simple. Most people just don't know what their pre-acquisition activities should look like. We are going to change that in this book.

It's not the governments job to help you figure out this market. "But Mike, there are programs for small businesses and small business advocates at the agencies. Isn't it their job to advocate for me?" Yes, part of their job is to advocate for small business. But it's not their job to hold your hand or spoon-feed you opportunities.

You still have to be proactive about educating yourself on how to run your business, identifying your top agencies, the nuances of government contracting, and so much more. This is your job. Don't wait around for the government to do this because they won't.

Your revolutionary widget or service. About half a dozen times a year, I get a call from someone who has invented a revolutionary widget or service. Their assumption is that because this thing is revolutionary, they can bypass all normal contracting procedures and land a sole source contract. Sure, it's possible, but it's not the norm.

The government is fairly resistant to change. When they do decide to make a change, it takes time. If they don't have a budget line item already established, it takes more time.

When thinking about your revolutionary idea, you have to determine if the government is already spending money on a similar item, whether they can simply reallocate those funds, or if they need to submit your items in the next budget cycle. The answer to this question alone could determine if you will sell your products/services in the next six months or if it's going to take eighteen to twenty-four months.

My point - new products and services often take time. The more "revolutionary" your product or service, the more time it will likely take. There are few exceptions to this.

The government is handing out sole source contracts. When I'm working with a client on their strategy, I don't even bring this up unless the client does. Just because you have your SBA WOSB or 8(a) certification doesn't mean the government is going to give you a sole source contract.

Do companies win sole source contracts? Absolutely! However, there's a lot of work that goes into making this happen. Some of that work is on your side. The majority of the work is with the contracting officer. That effort is called paperwork. The government has a lot of paperwork and they move slow.

During your research phase, you should review past contracts awarded by your target agencies. Look to see what percent were sole source. Some agencies love this method and will be happy to have that conversation with you. Some don't. Do your research. Ask your small business folks at the agency and the contracting officers if this acquisition method is something they would be open to using in the future.

You need a bid-matching system. Bid-matching systems connect to all of the free government systems. Their number one benefit is that they provide somewhat of a one-stop-shop for all the data you need to track down your buyers, do research on an opportunity, and ultimately bid on an opportunity. Yes, they do more than that, BUT the main reason people pay for these systems is to locate opportunities.

I've been in this market for 20+ years. I believe I've logged into dozens of the paid bid-matching systems. I like them. I think many have value. I also think many of them are ridiculously priced. You would think that with hundreds if not thousands of systems in the market, the price would be reasonable. You would be wrong.

Here's my other gripe about these systems. They are NOT one-stop-shops! Many of my clients that use these systems still need to access the free systems for more information.

So, if they aren't one-stop-shops and they are super expensive, why do so many people pay for them? Three reasons. 1) They are told they need them. 2) They don't know how to use the free systems. 3) People like the user interface. That's it. People are literally spending $10 to $15K per year on a system like this because they think it's easier. Yes, they are another tool in your bag. Just make sure you understand what value they provide.

You have to be in D.C. to sell to the government. I've been working on government contracts since 1999. In all that time, I've never lived in D.C. The first company that I worked for actually made me commute to D.C. from St. Louis for nearly two years. In those two years, I had less than ten face-to-face meetings with customers or partners. I still won millions in government contracts. I used the phone and email for 95% of my conversations.

I've worked from home since 2002. I'll never go back to working in an office. I'll never move to Washington D.C. There's just no reason. If there is one positive from 2020, it's that the whole world began the journey of understanding how to work from home and how to work from anywhere in the world.

This doesn't mean that it isn't beneficial to occasionally travel to D.C. In fact, for the right meeting with the right government buyer or teaming partner, I would highly recommend you make the trip. You just don't have to live there and you don't have to open an office there in order to be successful in selling to the government.

You can't have nine core competencies. I'm going to try to make this rant brief. You can't "specialize" in nine different things. I can't tell you how many times over the last few years I've received a capability statement that has janitorial services, cyber security, and a myriad of over unrelated services on it.

My question is always, HOW? How is it possible that you are an expert at nine different things? The truth is that you have experience with nine different things. You may not be an expert at any of them. But, you have to choose. A capability statement with nine core competencies will also generate an eye roll from a contracting officer.

When you enter the government market, you need to pick ONE thing to sell to the government. In most cases, it's the thing that you are best at. This should be your focus. This is your flagship product or service.

How do you go about picking the ONE thing? There's a couple of ways. First is evaluating what you really want to sell. I often ask the question, "what do you want to be when you grow up?" I know it sounds a little silly, but the heart of the question is really important. What do you want yourself and your company to be known for? Sometimes, this is all you need to determine what you should sell.

In some cases, a business owner is torn on what they want to sell. In these cases, we look at the data. A few simple searches in SAM and USASpending.gov can help point you in the right direction. You can quickly see where the government is spending money and who is spending that money. Then you can decide, based on the data and your gut feel, which direction to go.

My final piece of advice. Don't get tied to anything out of the gate. Pick something and give it six months to a year. If you don't like what you are selling, switch to something else. You need to love what you do. Fortunately, the government is a big market with a lot of needs. You can successfully transition to another product or service if you don't like your original choice.

Chapter 3.
Why the Middleman Strategy is a Scam

What is the middleman strategy? Simply put, the middleman strategy is a concept where you act as a broker between a supplier of products and/or services and the government. In this situation, you would take a cut of the contract and not have to do any of the work. At least, that's how this is portrayed on social media.

Why is it such a hot topic right now? A lot of people have discovered that government contractors struggle to win contracts. Course creation is also a hot service business. Put the two together and you have courses targeting government contractors. In my opinion, the middleman concept is attractive for marketing purposes. That's why people are creating courses that target this niche with this strategy.

At a high level, middleman marketing targets folks that don't really have a business, are probably working a job, and want an "easy" side hustle. Personally, I believe that's false adverting. But, it does sell a lot of courses.

A lot of the marketing I see talks about how easy this is and how you just need to look at what the government is buying and then sell that to them through quotes and bids. They make it sound like all you need to do is bid on the contract you want and you will win. If you've been in this market for any length of time, you know this isn't true. Strong companies in this market win anywhere from 20% to 60% of their bids. However, the industry average is closer to 10%.

What are the facts? First, there are rules in place that limit subcontracting. These rules were put in place to PREVENT pass-through situations - otherwise known as the middleman strategy. When the government awards YOUR COMPANY a contract, they want your company doing the majority of the work. That's why they awarded your company the contract. They don't mind if you subcontract a portion of the work, but they expect you to do 51%. That's the general rule. Exceptions apply, such as with general and specialty construction. Look up the limitations on subcontracting in the Federal Acquisition Regulations (FAR) to learn more about exceptions.

Besides the limits on subcontracting, there are several other holes in this strategy. Here are three more that you need to consider before trying the middleman strategy.

The first challenge is bidding on random RFPs. If something is on SAM and that's the first time you heard about it, it's likely wired for another company. If it's significant in size, you likely need past performance to win it. If it's small, (under $10K), it likely won't even show up on SAM until it's awarded, if at all. This means you are chasing your tail bidding on a lot of opportunities and not winning.

The best way to win contracts is by getting to know the customer. You won't do that just chasing RFPs. You have to pick up the phone and talk to contracting officers and program managers. You also need to build relationships with prime contractors and work as a subcontractor in order to gain past performance.

The second challenge is picking a niche. This goes back to the marketing of this strategy. You can't just bid on anything because it's cool or you think you can make a lot of money on it. Does it happen? Yes, but don't bet on it. You need to know about the products and services you sell. Here's a brief example of why this is important. One of my first coaching consultations was with a guy who had just won his first contract. He was super excited and terrified. He had just won a $65K contract for toilet paper. I asked why he was terrified. He said he didn't know anything about toilet paper. He had seen the RFP and went onto the Sam's Club (Walmart) website to get a price. He marked it down 10% thinking he could get a deal on the TP from Sam's Club.

I was, for lack of a better term, completely dumbfounded.

As you can imagine, there were a ton of issues with this thinking. First off, he didn't have a relationship with Sam's Club. Second, Sam's Club couldn't source that much TP in the timeframe requested by the government. Third, he couldn't find another vendor to supply the TP. And finally, he was running out of time. The government wanted this in less than 30 days (because he promised he could deliver in 30 days) and he only had 15 days left to deliver. He wound up contacting the contracting officer and backing out of the contract. To my knowledge, he's never won another contract with that agency or anyone else.

If you don't understand a product or service and don't have a relationship with a provider, you are creating an unnecessary learning curve in your business. You are better off focusing on something you know where you already have established relationships.

The third challenge is vendor relationships. As you can see from my previous example, you don't make promises that you can't keep. If you don't know how to deliver a product or service and you don't have the right relationships, you are doomed to fail. Even if you do have the right relationships, a lot of companies aren't willing to give you 51% of the contract while you sit back and do nothing. Are there exceptions? Sure, but those are rare.

The last thing you are probably wondering is if the middleman is a viable strategy or just smoke and mirrors. This strategy can work, but it's not best practice and it's often not scalable. I've seen it work best in the construction industry where the middleman is acting like a project manager or general contractor. In these scenarios, the middleman is getting 51% of the contract value to meet the regulations and the sub was willing to do the work for a negotiated rate. What usually happens is the middleman reverse engineers the quote. They find a sub willing to do the work, negotiate the best price possible, and then add enough for project management on top to meet the minimum 51%. As you can imagine, this often makes it hard to be competitive on price. It also makes it difficult for the subcontractor(s) to perform and complete the work.

The other strategy that works really well is the VAR strategy. However, that's not a hands-off strategy. You MUST add value to the contract. Think technology products for a moment. If you have a client that is buying a few Dell servers, they could buy them from you if you have a VAR agreement with Dell and then your company could install and set them up for the client. That's a value add to the customer. And guess what, Dell doesn't want to do that work. They just want to sell the servers.

In the example above for Dell servers, that isn't a side gig. The government isn't going to allow you to come in on nights and weekends to install the servers because you have a 9 to 5 and can't perform during business hours. Working with the government is a full-time gig.

As far as exceptions go, the main exception to you having to do 51% of the work is when your sub has the same socio-economic (also known as similarly situated) status as your company and the contract. For example, if the contract is an SDVOSB set-aside and both your company and your sub are SDVOSB; your subs work counts toward your 51%.

The percentage of work is also different for construction. For construction, you need to perform 25% of the work. If your company is part of a joint venture in an 8(a) mentor protégé relationship, the protégé must do 40% of the work.

There are also exceptions when the contract is under the simplified acquisition threshold (currently $250K) AND the contract is full and open. Again, refer to the Limitations on Subcontracting to learn more about the exceptions.

One final point to consider. It's a lot of work to win a government contract. Why would you want to work your butt off for a small portion of a win? Especially when you consider that winning the contract is the hard part. Performing the work is the easy part.

Here's a little math to drive home my point. Assume you have a 10% win rate and you are bidding on contracts with an average value of $100K with a 10% margin. How many contracts do you have to win in order to profit 100K? In this example, you have to win 10 contracts. 100K times 10 contracts equals 1M in revenue. Your profit is 10% or 100K. That sounds doable. But remember, you only have a 10% win rate. So, the real question is, how many contracts do you have to bid to win 10? The answer is 100! 100 contract bids multiplied by a 10% win rate is 10 contract wins.

In this scenario, you have to bid on two contracts a week. That math gives you a week off for Christmas and a week off for Thanksgiving. This assumes you can even find two contracts per week to bid on. It assumes that everything falls into place so that you can use a combination of exceptions so you don't have to perform the work. The odds just aren't in your favor.

But, what if instead of using the middleman strategy, you use a regular business strategy where YOU do the work and earn 30 to 40% profit margin? How many contracts do you have to win to get to 100K in profit? On the low end (30% margin), you will need three and 1/3 contracts. Since you won't win 1/3 of a contract, let's just say four contracts. This means you need to bid on just 40 contracts in order to win four. Four contracts at 100K equals 400K in revenue. With a 30% profit margin, you will earn 120K profit.

In the example above, you will increase your profit by 20K and only have to respond to 40 RFPs/bids. That's a 60% reduction in RFP responses and an increase in revenue. It's also less than 1 RFP per week.

If you are anything like me, the math alone makes a case to not consider the middleman strategy. But hey, it's really appealing on social media.

Chapter 4.
Identifying and Avoiding Con Artists

I need to start this chapter by saying I'm sorry to anyone who's ever been ripped-off by a government "expert." I'm not exaggerating when I say that I can't tell you how many horror stories I've heard of someone being scammed for a five-figure lump sum or anywhere from $10K to $40K per month for business development services.

If you think you are smarter than that and would never be scammed, think again. Some of the brightest people that I know have spent tens of thousands of dollars with the wrong people because they were new to the market and the con artist said all the right things.

In fact, that's at the heart of being a great con artist. They gain your confidence. It's right in the name. Once they have your trust, they can string you along for months.

Let me tell you two quick stories. The first is probably one of the wildest things I've heard in the last 20 years. Someone told me they hired a guy who said he knew every contracting officer at all the agencies they were targeting. He told them he was "close friends" (which was sort of true) with all of these folks and could get them meetings quickly. And he did. Or so they thought.

After a couple of the meetings didn't go anywhere, the client started pushing him about a contract. They were entering month five of his consulting agreement and still hadn't won anything. The consultant kept reassuring the client that it was just a matter of time.

On the next call with a contracting officer, the client started grilling the CO and she broke. She admitted to the client that she wasn't actually the CO. She was the consultant's girlfriend pretending to the be the CO. The client would later learn that ALL of the "COs" he had spoken to were actually family and friends of the consultant pretending to be contracting officers. This client had wasted thousands of dollars on this fake consultant.

My second story is a VERY common story. It's happened hundreds if not thousands of times. So, beware if someone like this ever approaches you.

I was onboarding a new client who had recently fired a retired General. They were paying this person $10K per month for business development services. Over the course of nearly a year, they had only been introduced to a handful of prospects. There were a ton of promises made and none kept. Did the General actually know everyone that he introduced the client to? Yes. He actually did. That was the problem. Everyone hated this guy and basically blacklisted him and the company he was working for. They figured any company that would hire this guy is probably just like him and they didn't want anything to do with either of them.

If you can be scammed by a former General, you can be scammed by anyone. Which leads me to an important point. I don't know if this General knew he was hated. Maybe he did, and maybe he didn't. In this case, I tend to think he knew something was wrong. At the heart of every scam is a scammer who KNOWS they can't deliver. In fact, their only intention is to string along the client as long as possible.

There are also situations where consultants aren't as good as they think they are, but they truly care about you. This falls in the category of overly optimistic, but not a scam. It's in your best interest as a business owner to put metrics in place to measure the progress of these relationships so that you aren't strung along for months without any meaningful or tangible results.

There are also times when you hire a company and it's just not a fit. This often happens when there's miscommunication about deliverables and/or a personality conflict. This usually isn't a scam. It's just an unfortunate situation. You can tell if it's a scam or not based on how the provider responds. If they truly try to make the situation right or they offer a refund and/or additional products or services to compensate you, that's a clear sign that they are acting in good faith.

A Few Ways to Spot a Scammer

1. If it sounds too good to be true, it likely is.
2. They say that you are going to see fast results.
3. The company doesn't have a website or doesn't have photos of their people on their website or social media. They are also using a Gmail or some other free email account instead of an actual domain with their company name.

4. They have had multiple company names in the last few years. This is often a sign that they had to shut down a company due to lawsuits or other factors and are in an endless loop of opening new companies so they can hide their true intentions. Another similar scenario is that they've just started their business or have some reason why they recently started a new LLC. Some reasons are legitimate, but use caution if their reason smells like B.S.
5. Nothing on their social media backs up what they are telling you. If they are awesome, there will be some social proof.
6. The don't have real references. If their references are first names without company names, something is wrong.
7. They are in a hurry to get the deal in place because of a contract you are going to miss out on.
8. You can't find their address anywhere! This should be easy to find.
9. They aren't registered for business in their state. You should be able to perform a simple search with their secretary of state to confirm they are registered as a business.
10. They promise the moon. Not only is it going to be fast, but they are going to make you a multi-millionaire.
11. They easily get combative when you question the process, results, or anything about them. Questions are good. If someone is a good person with your best interest in mind, they will welcome questions.
12. Their agreement with you doesn't give you a reasonable way to terminate the agreement. They are going to get their money no matter what.

What to Look for in a Reputable Coach or Consultant

1. They have a social media presence. It doesn't have to be huge, but they are making a decent effort to be consistent and interact with others.
2. They have a professional website.
3. They have professional contact information. Email, phone, etc. No google voice. Their address is easy to find.
4. They have real references. Recent clients that you can Google and confirm as real individuals with companies that are registered in SAM.
5. They want you to be comfortable before moving forward.
6. The price is reasonable based on their level of expertise and accolades. Note, you are going to pay more for a coach on the RSM Federal team given our track record of $14.6 billion in client contracts and the demand for our services.
7. Their expectations are reasonable and they can articulate with a degree of accuracy what you should expect during the course of your engagement.

How to Get Out of a Bad Situation

What should you do if you find yourself in a situation where you feel like you are being scammed or were recently scammed? First, if you are currently in a situation where you are actively being scammed, STOP PAYING THEM. If they have an iron clad agreement with you, you may need to contact an attorney to look at your options.

Depending on the situation, you probably need to confront them. You can do this easily by asking to sit down and *discuss their progress*. Before meeting with the consultant, sit down and make a complete list of your concerns.

During the meeting, be sure to address all of your concerns. If you don't feel 100% comfortable during or after your meeting, trust your gut. If this relationship is going to keep you up at night, you need to terminate it. Ask to terminate it in good faith. Again, seek guidance from an attorney if the contract appears to be iron clad or if you are not sure how to proceed.

In situations where you feel the consultant is clearly scamming you and you have evidence to that fact, you are also going to want to report them to the better business bureau as well as any state or federal licensing bodies if they have a license or certification of any kind. Again, you may want the advice of an attorney for the best course of action.

In some cases, you may decide to sue them. This really depends on the amount of money you are out and how bad you want to fight. There's an old saying that the only people that win in a lawsuit are the lawyers. The stress alone is enough for most people to avoid any type of lawsuit. Use your judgement and at a minimum consult with a colleague, coach, mentor, or even family member before going down this road.

Chapter 5.
Is Government Contracting Right For You?

You have probably heard that the government buys everything. And to a degree, that is true. The government buys a lot of stuff. In fact, I'm regularly amazed at some of the things I've seen the government purchase over the years. For example, did you know that the government buys pianos? I didn't know this. It's not a common item I think they would buy. But, occasionally they do.

Before you dive headfirst into government contracting, you need to find out if it makes sense for you to get into this market. What if the government only occasionally buys what you sell? What if the government only buys a small quantity of what you sell or they do it under a specific contract vehicle and you are locked out for five years?

These are just a few of the many questions you are going to read about in this chapter. I throw a ton of questions at you because whether you are brand new to the market or have been in the market for fifty years, a lot of people have never thought through all of this. Each question is a decision point that can influence your strategy.

You need the facts (data) before you jump into this market. Regardless of whether they buy a little or even a lot of what you sell, this journey is going to take time, energy, and resources.

When I'm looking at the data of who buys what you sell, I want to see significant purchase volume. That volume should be in the multi-millions (300M+) or even better, in the billions over the last three to five-years.

If the data does not show me multi-millions in government spend, I'm going to seriously question why you are getting into the market. Low volume data indicates that this is going to be a hard market to get into. In this situation, even if you break into the market and win "big," it may still only be a tiny amount. So, why chase the market? You better have a good reason.

A few other factors help determine if government contracting is a good fit for you. For example, what type of business are you trying to build? If you are looking for more of a laptop lifestyle where your focus is independence and not serious growth, this might not be a good market for you. The government wants to work with companies that are serious about what they do and who are dependable. That doesn't mean you can't run a lifestyle government business, but you need to have the proper expectations going into this journey and you likely need to self-perform on contracts, have a small team, and be prepared to be a subcontractor.

Another key factor, for product companies, is the type of product you sell. If you just invented some revolutionary new widget, that doesn't have an existing product category or doesn't replace an existing product, you are going to have a challenge breaking into this market. In fact, I often tell folks it's going to take two or more years for your first contract. There are exceptions to this, but you have to understand that new items take time.

Finally, do you have the attention to detail to make this work? Government contracting is all about paperwork. Even a small contract for $20,000 could be 25 pages of paperwork. Larger contracts can be upward of 100 or even 300 pages just to write a proposal in response to a Request for Proposal (RFP). Those larger contracts tend to have dozens of requirements. You have to ensure that your proposal speaks to every single requirement or you won't be compliant and your proposal won't even be considered. If you are not detail oriented, someone on your team better be.

How Big is the Market for Your Core Products/Services?

Now that we have considered the cautionary pieces, we get to do what I consider the fun part. We are going to dive in and do some research about your products/services.

I typically start my research by identifying two to three NAICS codes for your primary products/services. A NAICS code is the North American Industry Classification System code that identifies your products or services at a broad level. The reason I search on this first is because it's the standard code used by contracting officers when they create an RFP.

You will also hear the term PSC Codes. PSC codes are Product Service Codes. They are more granular than NAICS codes. They are used in addition to NAICS in some cases. And that right there is a lesson you need to understand about government contracting. You are dealing with people. And people have preferences that don't necessarily make sense. I've seen contracting officers use the wrong NAICS simply because that's what they've used for years and that's what they want to use. They are also human and make mistakes.

Let's get back to identifying your NAICS. Start by listing a few keywords that identify your products/services. Once I have a few keywords for your products/services, I often just Google search for the keyword and the word NAICS. My search will look like this, *"keyword* NAICS." That is often all I need to do to find a NAICS code. Then I repeat the process for the rest of my keywords. You will often discover that several keyword searches turn up the same NAICS. That's fine. It just means less NAICS to search in later steps and that the keywords fall under that NAICS.

If I can't find what I'm looking for with a simple search, I will often use https://naics.com/search. This website is really good for finding NAICS codes. One of the things that I like about it is that you can search by keyword and if that keyword shows up in multiple NAICS, you will get a list of all of them. If there are multiple NAICS with your keyword, write down all that apply and save these for your research phase.

If you don't know what keywords to use, one of the easiest tricks to finding this information is to look at your competitors. Most people know at least one or two companies in their industry that are chasing government contracts. Go visit their website and look for a government or industries tab. On that tab, they will either have their NAICS listed on their website or they will have a download available for their capability statement. Download this document and review it for their NAICS.

If your competitor does not have a website or doesn't have their government information listed on their website, you can still do some competitor research on them. You will need a SAM.gov account to do this. You can create one for free.

Once you have your SAM.gov account, do a search on your competitor. Use SAM.gov's Entity Search section to find the competitor and their profile. The web version of the profile is limited. I suggest downloading the entire profile. It will be a few pages in a PDF. Once you have that downloaded, you will see all of the NAICS and PSC codes that company has listed in their profile. Now you can pick and choose which ones are the most appropriate for your company.

I have one final trick for you to lookup your NAICS. Visit USASpending.gov. You don't need an account to access the data on this website. Click on Search Award Data and then enter your search criteria into the filters section on the left side of the page. For the time period, click All Fiscal Years. Then, scroll down to Recipient and enter in the name of your competitor. Then scroll to the bottom of that page and click search. If your competitor has won any contracts, those contracts will show up here. Click on the name of your competitor and that will bring you to their USASpending profile. About halfway down the page you will see the NAICS and PSC codes that they have been awarded contracts under.

What I love about this is that you see what NAICS/PSCs they are actually winning work under. This will help you prioritize your search and it will show you WHO their top clients are. This is all great information for your research phase.

Who Buys What You Sell

We have a great in-depth training on this topic in Federal Access. Joshua Frank does a deep dive into SAM.gov as well as a few additional websites to show you how we do this research for our clients.

Now that I have my NAICS, I'm going to turn my attention to propensity. Propensity is researching who buys what I sell, how much they buy, how often they buy, and which, if any, contract vehicles they may use. I use a combination of searches that start with USASpending.gov and SAM.gov. I initially just want to see at a high level if there's enough volume for me to do a more granular search. There are three reasons why I start with USASpending. 1) The website is fast. Once you use SAM.gov you will fully appreciate what I mean by this. 2) The user interface is super simple and visual. 3) I can adjust my searches on the fly. If I want to add or take away criteria, I can do it right on the same page. I don't have to go back into my reports and start all over…which is what you have to do with SAM for the most part.

Once you are on the USASpending.gov website, click on Search Award Data. I typically start with the last three to five fiscal years and check those boxes. I'm just looking for a snapshot of data for the last few years.

If place of performance is going to be a determining factor for you, I suggest clicking on the location section and entering in the place of performance information. This can be states, countries, etc. Add all of the locations that are relevant. If you can perform work anywhere, there's no need to select anything for this field.

Next up is your NAICS. Start with just one NAICS and then submit your search. The results will be in table form. At the top of the page, click on the Time tab. This will show you a bar graph of the buying trends for this NAICS. You just want to make sure the trend is either consistently increasing or pretty consistent. What you don't want to see is a downward trend. It's okay if there's a dip in the buying, but that shouldn't be the norm. If the spend is consistent or growing, I move to the next step.

If you are concerned about geographic restrictions, click the Map tab and you will see a map of the United States. Hover over the states you can perform work in and you will be able to see the dollars being spent in those states. If the government is not spending enough volume in the states you can perform work in, you will need to evaluate if you can move forward or not. As long as there is significant volume, you can move to the next step.

At the top of the page, click on the categories tab. This will rank the spending for this NAICS by agency. This allows us to see which agencies are buying what you sell. There's also a sub-agency filter so you can see at a more granular level who is buying what you sell.

The last thing that I'm going to look at before moving to SAM.gov are the recipients. If you are on the Categories tab, you will see a dropdown that says "Spending by." The default on this is Awarding Agency. Change this to Recipient. This will show you who the vendors are. These are other government contractors who are winning work under this NAICS. You can use his information for a wide variety of reasons, but I primarily use it for the initial snapshot to see if there are a lot of vendors.

What I want to see are dozens if not hundreds of companies listed as vendors for my NAICS. Why? Because I want to know that this market has room for entry. If I pull this data and there's only three or four companies and one of them has 90% of the contracts, I know upfront that this might be a tough market to break into. Plenty of competition means that there's room for your company too.

Diving Deeper with SAM.gov's Data Bank

Once we validate at a high level that there's a market for what you sell, I typically move to the SAM.gov Data Bank for more granular details. A lot of companies don't like using SAM because of the interface. I get it. It's not pretty and it's a little difficult to learn. At this phase, most companies skip SAM and jump into a bid-matching system such as Federal Compass, GovWin, MyGovWatch, etc. This is probably a good time to tell you that there's literally hundreds of these bid-matching tools. There's probably about a dozen or so that are at the top of the industry. The big difference between these systems and SAM is how the data is organized and what capabilities it has for data management after you identify an opportunity.

Regardless of whether or not you use a bid-matching tool, I highly recommend that you learn how to use the adhoc reporting in SAM's Data Bank.

 We have a great 15-minute video in Federal Access called "How to Setup a SAM report and use a pivot table like a pro." The video will help you set up an adhoc search, teach you how to use pivot tables, and shows you how we go about identifying your buyers. If you do nothing else with SAM adhoc searches, learn how to set up a few simple reports so you know your way around the system. I think you will be blown away with how easy it is to use once you learn how to do it.

I have a handful of saved reports that I consistently use in SAM. Every time I onboard a new coaching client, I pull these reports to get a better idea of who their buyers are and where we should be targeting our efforts. The thing I like most about these reports is that once I have the data downloaded, it's in an Excel spreadsheet and I can use pivot tables to look at different scenarios. If you aren't familiar with pivot tables, you can learn more about them in the video I mentioned above.

My favorite fields in adhoc reports are the "prepared by" and "approved by" fields. There are a few other "by" fields, but these two are the ones you will want to focus on. Can you guess what these fields represent? If you guessed the contracting officer names associated with a contract, you guessed right! Having that data at your fingertips is worth spending the time to learn SAM. This information is NOT in USASpending.

Once I pull a report and organize it by the top agencies buying what I sell, I add the "approved by" field and BOOM! There's an instant list of contracting officers email addresses. I can have this report in my hands in under five minutes. That's how powerful SAM is.

I will caveat the above by saying that some agencies such as the Department of State don't identify contracting officer names as easily as other agencies. The Department of State will often have a first initial and last name or some other naming convention. That's okay. Simply add the solicitation number field to the report and then you can go back into the solicitation search for SAM and lookup that number. Once you find that solicitation, scroll to the bottom of the page and you will find the contracting officers name, email, and phone number. This process takes a few more steps, but it's all part of the research phase of determining who buys what you sell.

You can also use SAM to look up active solicitations. This is primarily how people know about SAM.

Where are the Opportunities?

I recently spoke with a client that is only licensed to operate in NY and FL. A quick search in SAM for his NAICS showed 34 active opportunities, but not a single RFP in NY or FL. Why is this important? If you are only licensed to operate in certain states or you are limited by distance, you may not have access to enough or any opportunities. This alone could make you decide to either not pursue government contracting or open your eyes to states where you need to be licensed to operate in. Depending on what you sell, it may take months to add the additional licenses, insurance, or approved sales territory to your business. If this is the case, you need to take care of those business logistics before pursuing government contracts.

Another example that I recently ran into is a company that is a reseller of appliances. Their sales territory is limited to Missouri, Illinois, and Kansas by the manufacturer. They had a common challenge that we uncovered. There was plenty of volume for them to enter the market, but a lot of the contracts were being run through a contract vehicle that was being managed out of Alabama and not part of their territory. This was important to know before they started chasing contracts for two reasons. The first was a territory issue. They simply needed to speak with their manufacturer to let them know this information to avoid conflicts down the road. Second, they needed to build relationships with the contracting officers in AL and not just the ones in their destination or place of performance states of MO, IL, and KS. In fact, it was more important for them to build relationships with the Alabama contracting officers than the ones in their own backyard since those COs were the ones managing the contract vehicle.

An important question you need to ask yourself is, "Can I support a contract anywhere?" If the answer is no, that will change how you search for opportunities. Are you limited by state, country, or some other location factor? Why are you limited? Is it because you have to be onsite to do the work and you don't have the workforce? Is it because you don't have the ability to recruit and put people on contract quickly? What are your limitations? I guarantee you have limitations; you just need to identify them so you can be smart about how you chase contracts.

One consideration that you should always have in the back of your mind is teaming with other companies to overcome geographic limitations. This is just one reason we constantly preach about building your teaming stable. A healthy teaming stable overcomes a lot of limitations and is usually the difference between winning and losing. More on teaming in Chapter 19.

Can You Sell Direct?

If your product or service is primarily bundled under larger contracts, it might be a challenge for you to break into the government market. It's not a NO, but you need to be aware of this.

An example of this could be cabling such as electrical or internet cabling. This is likely to be part of a larger contract or installation. A prime is likely going to be chosen to manage the entire project and cabling might be a smaller piece of a multi-million-dollar award. In this scenario, if you can't manage the whole project, you will have to subcontract.

There are also large IDIQ contracts that are either managed by one prime or a handful of primes. You may be required to register as a vendor/supplier with them.

Two big contracts come to mind when I think about this. The first is a major logistics contract. If you are in the trucking or logistics industries, you are likely aware of companies like Crowley Logistics that is a prime on a multi-billion-dollar logistics contract. In this situation, you have to register on their website and be approved as a vendor/supplier in order to bid on these contracts.

The second example of this is an Air Force maintenance contract for overseas military installations. This contract has about half a dozen primes. This is a smaller contract and as a result, the primes don't have a vendor/supplier website established. Instead, these companies built teams and prepared their proposal based on their teams. This doesn't mean you are locked out if you aren't already on one of their teams, but it does mean it's going to be a little more difficult.

Most primes, especially the large well-known system integrators; have a small business office with multiple small business representatives. If you find yourself in a situation where you need to sell through a prime or join an existing team that is managed by one of these companies, their small business office is your first stop.

These offices operate similarly to the way government small business offices operate. Their focus is to meet great companies that can help them be more competitive, fill gaps in skills and talent, and ultimately position them to win more business.

One of the benefits of starting with a company's small business office is that these folks are typically very receptive to taking your calls/emails. They also know how to navigate the thousands of contracts, people, and divisions in their company; allowing you to quickly identify who you need to speak to about teaming on specific contracts. They are also the point person in their company for meeting their small business subcontracting goals. This means it's part of their job to help you.

The SLED Versus the Federal Market

First off, what is the SLED Market? The SLED market is State, Local, and Education. These contracts are managed at what we call the "local level" as opposed to federal contracts that are managed at the agency or command level.

Think about this for a minute. Let's say your business does small concrete work. Think sidewalks and small jobs similar to that. You own two or three trucks and have a team of about ten people. In this scenario you may only want to sell locally. Maybe your service radius is sixty miles or less. What if you are in a rural area where there aren't any federal government buildings or military installations? In this situation, you may be limited to local municipalities and schools if you want to get into "government" work.

The challenge with a market like this is that each community in your sixty-mile radius has a different team of people that manage contracts. They are likely all using a different method to post opportunities, if they even post them anywhere. You mix in the politics of having to be involved in the community or part of the community to get preferential treatment and what you have here is a business model that might not be scalable. You might make a really nice living, but at some point, you will likely want to grow outside of your sixty-mile radius and you will have to start from ground zero learning how new communities do business.

In case you missed it, I'm not a fan of the SLED model. Does that mean it isn't a good business model? Absolutely not. In fact, for the right company, it can be perfect. I'm just not a fan primarily because of the complexities of having to learn how each state or municipality operate. There are a lot of companies that thrive in this model. It's just not my expertise and I'm not afraid to say that.

What I will say about the SLED model is that there are a lot of similarities to the federal model when it comes to the basics of business. You need to get clear on your market as well as who buys what you sell. Once you identify your niche, you have to get clear on your message which revolves around the value you provide. You need to learn how to position with your prospects before opportunities get into the acquisition phase and you will need to get educated on the RFP process. A lot of similarities.

One key decision point that will lean your company toward the SLED market over the federal market is your understanding and ability to work on contracts that are out of your geographic region. I've seen plenty of companies that only have one office, but staff positions in dozens of locations all over the country. If you don't understand how to do this, you will likely struggle in the federal market unless you happen to be located near several government facilities.

What I love about the federal market is the connectedness of the whole thing and how big the market is. Think about that. The federal government is this massive trillion-dollar market with millions of employees and contractors and yet it feels a bit like a fraternity. You make friends at jobs and conferences and everyone shuffles around to new agencies, but remain friends.

Once you do business with an agency, that past performance will make it easier to win more contracts within the same agency and the government as a whole. Once you learn how one agency works, it's rinse and repeat with other agencies. There are minor differences, but the federal government works very similar from agency to agency. And last, but not least, they all use the same procurement system - SAM.gov. This means you only need one system to access opportunities and historical data. It also eliminates the need for a state-level bid-matching system. If you do choose the SLED market, a bid-matching system might be in your future.

Unlike the SLED market, the federal government is also very familiar with companies not being local. They contract with companies all over the world. That mindset and lack of local politics is a massive advantage over a client that wants to "keep their business local."

The final decision point for me between SLED and federal is financial stability of your local area. A great example of this is the state of Illinois. As I write this chapter, I'm in transition, moving from Illinois to Tennessee. Illinois is broke and has a poor reputation when it comes to paying their bills. There are plenty of companies with unpaid invoices that are months overdue. You would think this only applies to state level contracts in Illinois, but that's not entirely true. If the funding for your contract comes from a state bucket or even if a portion of the funding comes from the state (which happens a lot with city level contracts), you could be waiting months to get paid. Companies go out of business all the time by not getting paid for work they've done.

On the flipside, Tennessee is currently projecting a $3.6-Billion-dollar budget surplus right now. If I'm picking between these two states to work, this is an easy decision. Do your homework on your state or the municipalities in your region before diving headfirst into a pool with no water.

My last comment on this is that you don't necessarily have to choose between these markets. Depending on your business model, you might be able to work in both. Just understand going in that there are nuances to both and in an ideal situation, you would have different people on your team assigned to these markets so that they can focus on their unique customer base.

Do You Have the Finances to Support a Contract If You Win One?

What would happen to your business if you won a contract tomorrow that required you to immediately hire ten new employees? Assume for a moment that you can easily find and hire these folks. Could you float their salaries for ninety days? Why ninety days? Because that's likely how long it's going to take to get your first invoice paid by the government. You may get paid slightly faster, but ninety days is a good estimate. What if something is wrong with your invoice and your payment takes longer than ninety days? Can your business handle that? Most small businesses can't float that many salaries for that long. This is a case where winning a contract could put you out of business if you aren't properly prepared.

The same is true for product sales. Depending on what you sell, whether you are the manufacturer or a distributor, you have product costs and shipping to consider. Do you have the cash to support a large contract? If not, you may want to focus on smaller opportunities. If there aren't smaller opportunities, you may need to consider credit lines with your bank or your suppliers.

My point is that winning a government contract is quite a bit different than a commercial contract. In the commercial market, you can ask for money upfront from your clients. It's extremely rare to ask for money upfront from the government. That's just not how they buy stuff. Are there exceptions to this? Yes. One of those is micro-purchases. Micro-purchases under $10K are often purchased on a credit card.

How Long is it Going to Take to Win Your First Contract?

This is a great question. The answer is that it depends on several factors. However, I want to give you a direct answer. It takes the average company, emphasis on average…It takes the average company three to five years to win their first major contract. I know what you're thinking. You've got to be kidding me? Nope. That's how long it takes the average company.

Think about that for a minute. The average company that doesn't know anything about government contracting, who doesn't know who their clients are, how they buy, or anything else related to government contracting other than the fact that the government is the largest buyer of goods and services in the world. They are literally starting from scratch in a world where they don't even speak the language. This stuff takes time.

But here's the good news. Reading this book and implementing the strategies and tactics in it, will get you there MUCH faster. My goal is to help you win your first contract in the next six months. It may not be a big contract, but it will be a start and you will be well on your way.

What other factors contribute to the speed of you winning your first contract? The first one is the maturity of your company. If you are a brand-new company with no clients, it's likely going to take you a full six to twelve months to win your first contract. Maybe more. In this situation, you haven't even figured out what you are doing with your business yet. This should be expected. On the other hand, if your company has been around for a decade and has dozens or even hundreds of commercial clients, you likely understand your business model and your customer's needs. This will help you move much faster in the market.

Are you a niche company or all over the map? In 2020, I spoke to a few dozen companies that wanted to pursue *both* cybersecurity and janitorial services. There's nothing wrong with either business model, but both under one roof doesn't make a ton of sense. If you are all over the map, you are going to have to choose an area to focus on. You need to fine tune your messaging, marketing, and sales approach. You can't do that if you don't know who you want to be when you grow up. If you've already got this figured out, you're going to move much faster in this market.

Are you trying to sell a common product/service OR are you trying to pitch something brand new to the market? The government doesn't like change. Even if your widget is revolutionary, it's likely going to take time to sell something brand new to the government. The commercial market is much more likely to take a chance on a new product and a new company than the government is. Think of the government as a late adopter. Another challenge for a new product/service is budgeting. If your widget isn't already covered in their budget and we are at the beginning of the fiscal year, you may have to wait twelve to twenty-four months to make any sales. If you sell a common product or service, the government likely already has that in their budget and the decision is not if they will buy, but when and WHO are they going to buy it from. This will likely speed up your entry into the market.

How strong is your pipeline? Are you just responding to opportunities on SAM.gov or are you creating opportunities by talking to the government and teaming partners? The quality of your pipeline is an absolute game changer for companies. If you are only responding to opportunities on bid sites like SAM, you will likely struggle to get your first win. But, if you are gathering information and talking to the government and teaming partners BEFORE opportunities are released to the public, your win rate will skyrocket.

How big is your team? Is it just you? Are you juggling sales and the delivery of your products and services? Are you going to have someone dedicated to sales, proposal writing, teaming relationships, etc., or is this going to be a part-time gig for someone on the team? Government sales takes a lot of time. If you don't have the time to commit to doing it right, you're often better on waiting until you do have the time or a dedicated resource on your team.

Do you know anyone in the market? This could instantly help you get a win. This business is all about who you know and more importantly, who knows you. If your neighbor is a government contractor, go talk to them. If one of your friends works for the government or another contractor, go talk to them. If someone in your family is in government or knows someone in a government role, GO TALK TO THEM! You don't have to try to sell them anything. Just go talk to them and see if they can point you in the right direction.

When I was just getting started, I would often call someone and say the following: "My name is Michael LeJeune and I'm new to selling to the government. Could you help point me in the right direction?" I can't tell you how many times someone said, "Sure, what questions do you have?" Over the years of asking that question, I've only gotten one "no" and one "it's not my job to help you." That's it. Two negative experiences.

Over the years, I've also refined my approach so that when I call someone, it's clear that I've done my research and I'm not going to waste their time. This helps a lot, but my version of being lost and asking for help will still work.

How large is your market? This is an interesting one. The average company that calls me is trying to sell a fairly common service or product. Think technology, security, building maintenance, environmental remediation, etc. In these situations, the government is literally spending hundreds of millions or even billions of dollars on these services. I LOVE these industries because there's a lot of volume and that means there's room for new companies.

Occasionally someone will call with something that the government doesn't buy a lot of. A recent example of that is a blind company that I ran into at a networking event. While the government has purchased quite a bit of blinds over the years, they don't typically replace them very often. So, on a national level, the numbers are small and somewhat sporadic. Blinds aren't a consumable that need to be purchased every month or year. To make it a bit more complicated, this company was a franchise and could only sell to a limited territory. It would be one thing if their territory was California, New York, Chicago, Texas, or Florida where the economy in those areas is literally bigger than some countries. But, that was not their territory. Their territory was East Tennessee, an extremely small market. My advice, don't waste your time looking at the Federal government. In fact, even the SLED market might not be for you. Stay focused on the commercial market.

Finally, do you have the resources (time, finances, people) to float your company for 6 to 12 months? I'll say this again. Government contracting is not a side gig. It's a fulltime job. If you can't dedicate a fulltime resource to government sales, it's going to take a long time to win your first contract. That doesn't mean you shouldn't pursue it. It just means you need to go into this with your eyes wide open so you know what to expect.

Chapter 6.
Procurement Readiness

If you are new to government contracting, you've probably heard the phrase, "procurement readiness" a million times. Procurement readiness is nothing more than getting your business and yourself ready to do business with the government. This chapter covers six basic areas of procurement readiness.

 If you want additional resources on getting started: See the "Corporate Strategy Checklist" in Federal Access. It lists 43 items you need to do to be procurement ready.

1. Registrations

SAM.gov. If you are not registered in SAM, you need to do this ASAP. A few years ago, SAM registrations could be done in an hour or less. Today, I've seen issues with the system that can cause registrations to take weeks for approval. Unlike in past years, you now have to submit legal documentation proving your company exists. Get started on this immediately.

You will need your key business information such as EIN, business address (no virtual addresses allowed at this time), and other key business information such as your NAICS, PSC codes, etc. Don't worry if you don't know all of this initially. You can and should update your SAM profile regularly.

Once you are registered in SAM, you will receive your SAM Unique Entity Identifier (UEI). The UEI replaced DUNS numbers several years ago. This means you don't have to go to Dunn and Bradstreet to request a DUNS before starting the SAM registration process. Once your registration is approved, you will automatically receive your Commercial and Government Entity Code (CAGE) code. Your CAGE code is a five-character alphanumeric code, provided by the Defense Logistics Agency (DLA) that is used to track and manage Defense contracts. Your UEI and CAGE code need to be listed on your capability statement.

SBA Website. If you are small, go to sba.gov and register for an account. You are going to need this along your journey for small business certifications and to manage your DSBS profile.

SBA DSBS. The Dynamic Small Business Search website is a place that contracting officers and contractors use to search for companies. If you are small, you need to make sure you are registered here once you are registered in SAM. The only way to create your DSBS profile is through SAM.gov. As you're registering in SAM, don't skip the section that says, "Do you want to complete your DSBS profile now?"

Login.gov. I had to take a deep breath before writing about this one. You will understand after you set this one up. Several government websites use identity verification websites like Login.gov to confirm your identity. SAM.gov is one of those websites. The most frustrating part of this is often getting a clear picture of your driver's license. I've seen this process run smoothly and I've seen the website crash ten times in a row before it works.

SLED Websites. If you are planning to work in the state, local, and/or education market, there are procurement websites that you need to look up for each of those. A simple search such as: TN Procurement Website (for my state), should lead you directly to the site/s you need to register on.

One of the reasons that I don't like the SLED market is how decentralized the procurements are. If you sell to local municipalities, you likely need to register on a different website for each of them. This means you might be monitoring a dozen or more websites at any given time. If you sell to the education market, each school district, university, and private school is likely to have their own system. This is one of the few instances where a bid-matching system might be your best friend. The right system will consolidate all of this information, from multiple buyers, into one website.

SLED websites are also typically the place you need to register for state level certifications. This will usually be marked on the website as DBE certifications. These include minority owned, woman owned, persons with disabilities, service-disabled veteran owned, and small business enterprises.

DIBBS. If you plan to sell products to the government, you may want to consider an account on DIBBS. This is DLA's Internet Bid Board System. DLA purchases a LOT of products for the government this way.

ARC. If you plan to sell to the NSA, be sure to check out the ARC. This is NSA's Acquisition Resource Center.

Agency specific websites and approved vendor lists. Depending on who you are selling to, an agency, office, or military base, they may have a specific website or email address listed on their website for interested vendors. Simply follow their process to become listed on their approved vendor list.

2. Certifications

Now that you are registered, you need to start working on your certifications. It's important to note that many certifications are going to require the same information over and over again. With this in mind, it's important to create a simple document archive for certifications in order to quickly and easily access this information.

Initially, focus on learning what your company is eligible for. Are you WOSB, SDVOSB, 8(a) (minority owned), live and work in a HUBZone, etc. If you are planning to target the VA and are eligible for SDVOSB, your Veteran certification is a priority. If not, and you are eligible for WOSB, that is likely your priority. For minority and socially disadvantaged business owners, engage the market and wait a year before submitting for 8(a) certification.

A word to the wise. Review the eligibility requirements for the certifications you think you qualify for and make certain that you are 100% eligible. One of the key requirements for each certification is 51% ownership by the person who qualifies for the status. That person must own and be in full control of the business.

A pet peeve of mine is husbands that list their wife as the 51% owner of their company, in name only. If I wind up on a consult with a husband of a WOSB, one of the first questions I ask is, "Where's the W?" A lot of times, the answer is, "She's not involved much." That doesn't fly with me. You are either a WOSB or you're not. I'm not going to be party to lying about your status. I always tell folks in this situation that they either need to correct this issue by getting their wife involved or they need to withdraw their WOSB.

In fact, now would be a good time to introduce you to the False Claims Act (FCA). This is covered in the Code of Federal Regulations under 20 CFR § 356.3 False Claims. The gist is that the government can come after you and/or your business if you provide false claims such as being a woman owned business when you know you aren't a WOSB.

Last, I highly suggest putting a tracking system in place for your certifications. You likely won't get everything on the same day. You need to be able to track what certifications you have as well as when reporting or recertification is due.

In case you skipped the myth-busting chapter, understand that a certification or "status" is not a golden ticket. As I mentioned a few paragraphs earlier, if you are new to the market, please wait on getting your 8(a). You only get nine years. If you're not ready to succeed in this market, wait a year so you can maximize those nine years.

3. Product/Service Information

My recommendation is to start out with no more than three to five products and services. Pick one as your flagship product or service and focus your profiles and marketing information around that one thing. The other two to four things should support your flagship product or service.

Once you figure out your primary product or service, you need to determine your primary NAICS and PSC codes. Don't get stuck on this. It is important, but *don't overthink it*. You need NAICS and PSC codes for your profiles, capability statement, etc., but you can always change them as you go. Initially, you need a starting point for your research.

Once you know your products and services, you can look at pricing models. You've got to get sharp on how you price your products and services.

If you don't understand pricing, you won't understand how to make money in this market.

I'm not going to claim to be an expert on this. In fact, I hate working on pricing models. But it's important. That's why I often bring in a pricing expert to look over these models.

Pricing experts don't cost a lot of money. You can bring somebody in to help you develop a template for your products or services. That's usually all you need from them. You may check in with them every year or so to help you with your model to make sure you are on target, or help tweaking some numbers for a proposal. In fact, most pricing experts are great at looking up previous contract awards, analyzing your competitors pricing, and putting together competitive rates.

The next bullet item to consider is your differentiators. What differentiates your products and services from the rest of the market? Is it because you have special pricing? Is it because you're the manufacturer? Maybe you're the sole source. There's all kind of things that could differentiate why somebody would buy your products and services from you versus someone else.

It could be your speed to deliver. I've got a client that has a super power when it comes to recruiting. Their speed of recruiting and putting a butt in a seat is much faster than the average company in the market. The average company may take anywhere from six to eight weeks, or longer, to recruit a new position and they can do it in three to five days. That's a differentiator.

It could be the location that you serve. Maybe you have the biggest network in Ohio for servicing a particular type of product or service and you are THE company to hire when it comes to buying that in Ohio for whatever reason. That could be a differentiator.

The next thing is your past performance. Where have you sold this product or service in the past three years? Who have you sold it to? What were the scenarios? What did you actually do? How many users did it serve? How many locations? How many projects? You need to get clear about your past performance so you can build your marketing materials and prepare for proposals.

The government is all about proposals for the most part. There are some contracts that just get awarded. But in general, the government wants to see you fill out paperwork. Paperwork is in the form of an RFP or RFQ. When you're filling out a proposal or quote response, you are going to have to describe your past performance in detail. What did you do? How many units did you sell? How many FTEs did you have on the project? Who did you do the work for? What value did you provide? These are all important questions that you need to be able to answer.

You've got to be able to get granular about your past performance, and it's best to do that now while you're getting procurement ready. Doing this now will make you faster as you actually start chasing opportunities.

 We have detailed examples and strategies on communicating past performance in addition to several examples of proposals in the Federal Access Coaching and Training Platform.

4. Market Information

Do you know WHO buys what you sell? Do you know HOW they buy what you sell? Do you know their preferred contract vehicles and set asides? Do you know WHO they buy from today? Do you know how big your market is?

Those are just some of the questions you need to understand about the market. The good news is you can go into SAM.gov and pull reports on all of the questions that I just outlined for you. You can figure out who's buying what you sell, how they're buying it, who they're buying it from today; all that stuff is in SAM.gov's Data Bank.

Most people think the government, which is huge, buys what you sell, and they probably do. But, if you can zero-in and figure out exactly which contracting officers are buying it, you can build a targeted strategy around those folks. This will make it easier to gather information and intelligence on your top buyers in order to build relationships with them.

5. Marketing Materials

The main things you need initially are a Capability Statement, Capability Brief, and a Website with a government landing page. That's it! You will develop more materials later. This is just the starting point.

Your capability statement has all of your key corporate information. It's not something you need to overthink. Make it simple out of the gate by using one of our many templates in Federal Access.

One important tip, keep your Capability Statement to one page. Contracting officers barely have time to review one page. If your Capability Statement is more than one page, people aren't likely to review it.

Your website doesn't have to be complicated. In fact, there are several low-cost website builders like wix.com with simple templates to get you started. You can even make your first website based around your capability statement. Start from there. You don't have to get crazy and have a 50-page website. A simple one pager that scrolls from section to section is totally fine. If you can, make sure there's a PDF version of your capability statement that is easy to find and download.

That last piece of your marketing is your capability brief. This is a PowerPoint type presentation. It's a little bit more expanded than your capability statement. This is something that you will share with contracting officers, program managers, and teaming partners to introduce them to your company. It's also the starting point for capability briefings with government program managers.

6. Infrastructure

Your back office is one of the largest assets you have when starting your government contracting business. This includes vendor relationships, software, hardware, systems, processes, bonding, funding, vehicles, and much more.

KPI Dashboard: At the top of my infrastructure list is having a dashboard for monitoring your business. This is where you track all of your important KPI's. Our dashboard includes a list of all of our clients, how/where the lead was generated, what our retention rates are, profitability breakdowns, and plenty of other details. This allows our team to make financial decisions months and years in advance.

Vendor Relationships: When I think about infrastructure, one of the top things that I think about are vendor relationships. If you are selling products, do you have relationships with manufacturers and distributors? You don't want to wait until you have a proposal due before you have these key relationships in place. It's difficult to sign up as a vendor and get preferred pricing when you have a proposal due in 72 hours. You don't want to put your company or your vendor in that position.

You need your vendor relationships months in advance. It takes time to put contracts and pricing in place. Also, initially, you don't need 50 relationships. You likely need one or two.

Accounting and Payroll Systems: If you're already doing millions of dollars in commercial sales, you likely already have an accounting and payroll system in place. However, you need to ensure that you are using the right platform and that it's compliant for government contracting. Depending on the contracts you work on, you may also need to be Defense Contract Audit Agency (DCAA) compliant.

Human Resources: How do you recruit and on-board employees? How do you manage employee benefits? How do you handle employment issues?

All of these are good questions that you need answered. Many of the answers require a person and process to be in place.

Software and IT Systems: I can think of, off the top of my head, around 20 different software applications that we use in our business. One of the most important applications that we use is our CRM. Many of our clients use HubSpot. I've been on the free version for over four years and love it. You also need your email accounts, Microsoft Office, data/file storage systems, and a way to create invoices. You will also likely need a way to process credit cards.

We also use several systems and vendors to manage daily activity. We use Dropbox for file sharing. We have a hosting company that manages our website. We use Microsoft Outlook for managing email. I use Canva and Evernote on a daily basis. Many of our clients use SharePoint and other systems for collaboration. What software and systems do you need to run your business?

Bonding and Insurance: Depending on what you do, you may need bonding, you may need insurance. Those are all kinds of things that you need to make sure you have before you actually pursue a contract. Funding is another one. If you don't have a credit line or a loan to operate the business, you need to get those now instead of once you land a contract.

Processes: Everything in your business has a process. The challenge for most people is outlining what those processes look like. Whether it's sales, customer service, HR, or marketing, you can't improve something if you don't track it. You also can't ensure quality standards if you don't have a process in place. Processes help you better run your business. One of your assignments as a business owner is to make sure that every area of the business has a detailed process for its core activities.

Cybersecurity: I'm not going to get into the weeds on this. I simply want to bring to your attention the topic of Cybersecurity Maturity Model Certification (CMMC). The government has repeatedly kicked the proverbial can down the road on this topic several times. If I had a crystal ball, I would guess that this stays a bit of a mess for a while, but you need to be aware that the Department of Defense is pushing cybersecurity requirements on businesses. It doesn't matter if you are a tech company or a janitorial company. You are going to have some level of responsibility for protecting client data. Google CMMC as part of your action items from reading this book. Stay on top of the requirements.

Chapter 7.
Picking Your Niche

Picking a niche is a massive challenge for many government contractors. People tend to want to be a "full service" organization. And that's fine if all of your products and services are complimentary. It's not fine if they are not complimentary. No matter what you think, a company that sells cybersecurity and janitorial services...are not complimentary services. And yet, I talk to companies all the time that want to specialize in these two.

This is not just a start-up issue. I've talked with very mature companies that are $50 million in annual revenue who aren't sure what they do best or where they want to focus. It's the focus on a niche that allows them to scale from 50M to 100M and to increase profitability by 2, 3 or even 500% in some cases.

I'm not sure who coined the phrase that there are *riches in niches*, but they were spot on. The more you can focus your company around a single solution, the easier it is for everyone to pursue a common goal. The added benefit of a niche is that your company becomes REALLY good at it; you can charge more; and it becomes easier to beat your competition. This is why you will see a significant increase in profitability.

This begs the question - how do you choose your niche when there are so many options? I usually recommend looking at five areas to make this decision.

Disclaimer... These areas are just a guide to help you make a decision. Ultimately, it's going to be up to you to decide and commit to something.

1. The 80/20 rule

A simple way to come up with an answer for your niche is to look at the breakdown of your revenue. If you look at your revenue, you are likely bringing in 80% of your business from one product or service. The remaining 20% is likely a combination of several sources.

This is a great indication of what your company has learned to sell - as well as what your company has learned to deliver with excellence. It's rare that this is a fluke unless you're a brand-new business with just a handful of customers. If you are new, this might not give you the full picture of where you should niche, but it's often a great indicator.

2. Product or Service

If I look at what you are selling, there needs to be a flagship product or service. A lot of companies have complimentary services to the flagship. What I tend to do here is to look for the product or service that is going to be a gateway to selling the other services. For example, let's say your company provides building maintenance, janitorial, and landscaping services. Which one of those is likely to help you get a foot in the door the fastest with your ideal client? Also, which one of those will position your company for the other services? In this case, I would likely choose building maintenance. Why? Because it's more likely that the same customer will hire you to do janitorial and landscaping AFTER you do a good job on their building versus hiring you to work on their building after you cut their lawn.

Digging deeper into this example, which one of these services provides an ongoing opportunity to talk with your customer? Only the building maintenance service. The other services are so simple that they don't require a lot of communication with the customer. In fact, the landscaping example won't even get you in the building. So, in this example, go with building maintenance. Do a great job for a month or two and then ask the contracting officer or site supervisor for a capability briefing. That's when you talk to them about how you can help with the janitorial and landscaping issues you've observed while working on their building.

3. Your Background

Your background is VERY important. What do you already know? Let's use the building maintenance example again. If you've been in building maintenance, janitorial, and landscaping your whole life, you won't have a learning curve about the services that you are providing.

Where most companies go off the rails is that they will hear about a large vehicle maintenance or software development contract (which is outside their expertise) with their target agency and think that this is just another contract. They can simply hire someone to manage it.

That's correct in theory, but not in practice.

If you don't know anything about a product or service, you likely shouldn't consider it. It's nothing more than a shiny object that is distracting you from what you do best.

Another great example of this is a prospect that I spoke with yesterday. He found a solicitation on SAM for shotguns. He and a friend recently "opened" a gun store. What this really means is that they went through the process of getting licensed. They don't actually have a physical store with inventory and employees. In fact, when I questioned him, he's not running this business full time. He's a full-time project manager for a major defense contractor.

When I started grilling him about his project manager experience, a lightbulb went off. He realized that he has over 20 years' experience in this area. So, I asked the million-dollar question. Why not start a business that provides project management? There's no inventory. It doesn't require any reseller agreements, pricing issues, or shipping. While it is competitive, there's a lot more room for competition. There are only so many companies that sell Mossberg shotguns. That is going to be an extremely competitive market. And by the way, there's no learning curve for project management when you have 20 years' experience.

Avoid shiny objects by leaning on your background.

4. Your Passion

Be careful about this one. Just because you are passionate about something doesn't mean the government is buying it. We always start our research by looking at who buys what you sell and determining propensity (buying volume and frequency).

If the government is buying what you want to sell AND you are passionate about it, that could be a perfect niche for you. Some questions to consider: Are you already selling this product or service? Do you know how to package and price it? Do you have vendor relationships in place? Do you already have an in-depth knowledge of this topic? Is selling this going to ruin your passion for it? Depending on your answers, picking your passion might be the perfect route for you.

5. Just Pick Something!

This last option is a great fall back. When you aren't sure what to do, just pick something that checks several of the boxes mentioned above. It's more important to get started than it is to debate this to death.

If you get going and realize there's a problem with your niche (like the shotgun guy), simply change it! It's that easy.

Chapter 8.
Branding Yourself and Your Company

A great brand strategy will create an unfair top-of-mind advantage for your company. When someone thinks of a product or service, you want them to think of your company first. The best brand strategies understand the importance of branding its individual leaders and not just the company. In this scenario, when someone thinks of a product or service, they think of you (and your leadership team) AND your company first.

The heart of every great brand is operational excellence and that is only achieved by having a strong leadership team that lives and breathes the brand! When these pieces fall into place, you will create a seemingly effortless sales engine that powers the brand and creates INBOUND leads.

I speak to an average of 15 to 20 new prospects every week who want to work with our team of coaches. That's just shy of 2,000 potential clients every year. One thing that they all have in common is that they have been watching or listening to me for quite some time before we get on the phone. In fact, I can't tell you how often someone is "star struck" because they have been listening to my podcast for years. It's quite humbling.

Notice two things about what I just wrote. 1) I'm getting approximately 2,000 INBOUND requests per year from people interested in our services. 2) They've spent months if not years getting to know me. This means there's no selling on my calls. I ask a few questions, provide some guidance, and if someone wants to take the next step, **they ask me** to move forward.

I bet one of the things you are thinking is that B2G doesn't work that way. The government can't just buy from you because they know, like, and trust you. If that's what you're thinking, you are only partially correct. Depending on your status and the size of the contract, there are a TON of situations where the government *can* and *does* in fact buy this way.

Before we get into the concepts in this chapter, there are a few things I want to make clear.

Branding is a long-term strategic process.

Marketing is a short-term tactical activity.

These two are intertwined, but not the same. Branding is not your logo or stationery. Branding is the result of many activities geared toward creating awareness that you and your company exist as well as the value you provide. Branding is MUCH bigger than a logo.

In this chapter, I'm going to introduce you to four concepts and four tools that I've used to build my personal and company brand.

Brand Concept #1: Be the Best at What You Do

How do you become the best at what you do? The short answer is that this takes years. It also takes a lot of focus. You can't spread yourself thin and expect to be the best at anything.

We used to say that mastering any concept took around 10,000 hours or five years of work. This concept was made popular by Malcolm Gladwell in the book *Outliers*. However, there's a new concept that's popped up over the last few years called the 20-hour rule. This rule states that it takes approximately 20 hours of deliberate and focused practice to become reasonably competent at a new skill.

If it only takes 20 hours to become reasonably competent at anything, this means you can become great at anything in much less than 10,000 hours. You can put in 20 hours' worth of effort in a weekend if you are dedicated. This means you can get up to speed on anything fast! Then, you can take the next few years to master it.

The key in both scenarios is *deliberate effort*. You have to focus on your craft. This means eating and sleeping whatever you do. This kind of effort is not easy. In fact, it's quite hard. That's why so few people go on to create powerful brands. They don't have the passion or energy to deliberately focus on their craft.

In addition to deliberate effort, I've found that surrounding myself with other experts in my field to be critical to my development as a government contracting subject matter expert. I never want to be the smartest person in the room. I'm always looking to add to my knowledgebase and the only way to do that is to spend time with people who know things I don't know or have a different spin on something I do know.

And before you ask, I'm not worried about my "competitors" learning from me or trying to steal my ideas. My focus is on learning. I can openly share information without giving away my intellectual capital.

Brand Concept #2: Focus on Helping People

The number one reason I've been so successful in business is that I always provide value before asking for money. A great brand is customer centric. Enough said.

Brand Concept #3: Have a Big Vision

A great brand doesn't think small. Take Apple's initial vision: *A personal computer in every home.* That's billions of computers. Their current vision is *To make the best products on earth and to leave the world better than we found it.* Those are two bold goals.

Every company and every personal brand is based on what you want to accomplish. If you just want a nice side hustle (which is not government contracting), you are going to build your business one way. If you want everyone in the world who is a potential customer to buy your stuff, you are going to build your company very differently.

In 1984, Nike convinced Michael Jordan to sign a five-year 15-million-dollar contract to elevate their brand. Nike was a good company before this. They've never been the same since. Their current vision is *To bring inspiration and innovation to EVERY athlete in the world.* That's not a small task.

While their vision is big, you may have also noticed something important about both Apple and Nike's vision. They are both customer centric.

What's your vision for your company? Is it focused on excellence and your customer? If not, now might be a great time to reevaluate.

Brand Concept #4: Think Like a Gangster

I've watched my share of gangster movies over the years. I've noticed that the godfather (head of the organization) is always aggressive and business savvy. You don't become the godfather without talking a little smack and backing it up.

The godfather is not only strategic, but methodical in his approach. He is constantly looking at expanding the business and knows how to delegate (leadership). He moves quickly to build networks (alliances and relationships). He is relentless in the pursuit of his vision and doesn't tolerate bad apples who aren't on board.

If you are going to be successful at building your brand, you need to aggressively pursue your goals, constantly communicate your vision to the world, and be strategic and confident in your approach.

Tools for Branding

100% of our business comes from a combination of the following four tools. Someone will usually hear the podcast or pick up one of our books and then go down the rabbit hole of following us on social media and attending one of our speaking sessions online or at a conference. That's often how someone becomes one of our clients. Some clients start in reverse order by attending an event.

My point is that we have plenty of options online for someone to find us and get to know us. Have you ever heard the phrase, "people buy from people that they know, like, and trust"? One of the hardest parts of that sales equation is the KNOW part. People have to find out about you. They can't do that if you hide under a rock. You need tools you can use to broadcast your message.

Tool #1: Social Media

Social media is like a megaphone for your brand. Done properly, people will see and/or hear it and get to know you. My three favorite social media tools right now are LinkedIn, YouTube, and TikTok (in that order). Will TikTok get banned? Maybe, but as I'm writing this, it's not!

Here's a simple fact about social media. Your prospects and teaming partners use it. Everyone uses social media differently, but we all use it at some level.

Tool #2: Podcast

Would it shock you to learn that more than 241,000 podcasts debuted their first episode in 2022? We started our podcast in 2016 with no idea how it would impact our brand. Today, we have hundreds of thousands of downloads and a very loyal listener base. Most of the time when I meet someone at an event, the first thing they tell me is that they've been listening to the show for years.

Our podcast has significantly helped us with the Know portion of the sales equation, also in addition to the Like and Trust portions. With more than 300 episodes and roughly 150 hours of recordings, people have spent a significant amount of time learning about government contracting AND learning about us.

Tool #3: Books

The average person typically sells five to seven copies of their book. That's the total over their entire lifetime. Once you remove the obligatory purchase from your mother and a few friends, that likely means only one prospect will buy your book.

We are fortunate to sell hundreds every month. This isn't an accident. It's a combination of the work we do to build our marketing lists, social media, and our podcast.

The great thing about a book is that it adds a level of credibility that you just don't get from anything else. Imagine for a moment that two companies are competing for the same client. One company has a book and the other doesn't. Which one is going to win that battle most of the time? The one with the book.

Tool #4: Public Speaking

The first three tools are all self-promotion style marketing and people know that. This fourth option is when an organization or company does the promotion and you leverage their credibility. This is huge for your brand.

In our case, we speak at widely respected government conferences and online events. The mere fact that the organization has us on their agenda is a bit of a rubber stamp of approval. People realize that they don't just let anyone speak at these events. It's competitive and only the best topics and presenters are chosen.

This type of promotion is impossible to buy. The other factor that I love about this is that it's one to many. Even if you are in a small breakout room instead of the main stage, you can expect to be in a room with fifty people in your audience who all want to hear you talk about your topic. This leveraged approach is not only good for your business, it's a great allocation of time. It's a great way to accelerate your brand.

Chapter 9.
Social Media Strategy Considerations

When most people think about social media, they think about setting up profiles and posting one or two times per week. That is NOT a social media strategy. That's a casual relationship with social media. It doesn't matter which platform you choose, the platform algorithm does not like casual relationships. The goal of social media platforms is to keep users on their platforms as long as possible and they only reward users who understand this and work hard to help them achieve this goal.

This chapter is devoted to helping you understand the thought process behind a great social media strategy. Once you understand these simple components, you should be able to craft a simple and effective social media strategy that fits your brand.

Clear Goals

Like with anything in life, you need to have goals for your social media strategy. They don't have to be complicated, but they need to be specific. I often recommend choosing your platforms and getting them setup as your first goal. From here, set a goal to create a content plan. How many times per week are you going to post? What type of content are you going to post? How many times per day are you going to comment on other posts? When are you going to hit your first 100, 500, and 1,000 connections, followers, subscribers, etc.?

One of the best things about a goal is that it provides focus. A goal lets you zero-in on the activities required to accomplish the goal. This provides guardrails, that if used properly, will reduce distractions. Another great thing about goals is that they provide clear evidence that your strategy is working or it's not. You either hit the goals or you don't. If you don't have this feedback, it's easy to flounder on social media. Remember, the goal of social media is to keep users on the platform as long as possible. Any platform can be a black hole that sucks every moment of your day.

Authenticity

The thing that you bring to the table on social media is YOU. You are unique. While I truly believe in learning from others that have mastered social media, I don't believe you should mimic them. You need to put your unique spin on everything you do. Your personality should shine bright in your posts. People who share your personality traits will be drawn to you.

One of the things that I started sharing in 2023 was my time out on the lake. I regularly work from the lake and have found that it's a great place to shoot videos. I had no idea how many people would interact with me based on these simple boating videos. The feedback has blown me away. I've signed new clients based on those videos. I've had people reach out to me to tell me how those videos have inspired them to get back out on the lake. I've also made quite a few new connections and friends because of those videos.

People connect with my lake videos for several reasons, but the most important reason is that they see common ground between us. It's important for them to either be on a boat or out in nature. And that is all it takes to create a connection with someone. Common ground.

The other thing that everyone notices about my videos is that I'm usually in a hoodie or t-shirt and a ball cap. I'm a very down-to-earth simple guy. That comes across in my videos. But it also comes across in my podcast and when you meet me in person or over the phone. No matter where you meet me, I'm the same guy. What you see (or hear) is what you get. It's real and my people get that. I'm not for everyone, but my style stands out in a sea of suits and ties and bald white guys.

Quality Content that Educates

A post about your latest website update doesn't educate anyone. Similarly, a post about your updated capability statement doesn't educate anyone. What educates people? A short paragraph about your three big takeaways from a recent conference. A whitepaper that describes ten things to consider when implementing a corporate cyber security plan. A short video describing an aha moment that you had while implementing a new

CRM. Five stats you found going down a rabbit hole researching GSA Schedules. All of these things educate people.

If the focus of your content is on the people consuming the content and NOT yourself or your company; you will see your profile grow quickly, increase engagement, and have more success with your social media strategy.

Quantity

Quality is not enough! You need quantity if you want to get noticed and grow on social media. It's also important to note that you don't have to follow my model of multiple posts per day. However, one post per week isn't going to cut it. This goes back to having a casual relationship with social media. Daily posting is important. You don't have to post a new whitepaper or video every day. You can post a single sentence. Earlier today I posted this sentence: "We (me included) tend to spend too much time on insignificant decisions and not enough time on the big ones."

That simple post has kept my audience engaged, it's garnered a dozen likes, a few comments, and it spurred a friend to text and thank me.

People get overwhelmed when they hear about daily posting. But as I've just shown you, it doesn't have to be complicated. It just has to be thoughtful and intentional.

Consistency

I often see profiles that haven't posted in months. You aren't going to get any traction like that. You have to use your platforms. As I stated in the last section, your goal should be daily posting. However, you could start out weekly. You could start by writing an article every Tuesday. Then you could add a short text post on Thursday. In between those posts you could focus on commenting on other posts. That gives you a foundation to build on while you learn the platform.

The takeaway from this section is that you can't go weeks or months without posting and expect to get results.

Engagement

One of the things that is always on my mind is engagement. Whether it's asking a question or striking a nerve, I'm always thinking about generating a response. It can be as easy as saying, "please comment with your thoughts below." Initially when people start on social media, the focus is on the content. As you master that, your mindset should and will shift to generating engagement.

Engagement (likes, shares, and comments) are like pouring gas on an open flame. It increases your distribution (eyeballs) and accelerates your growth.

When your audience is small, you often have to prod for engagement. This means you are literally asking for it. As your audience grows, people will automatically engage with your content because of human nature. Your audience will basically train themselves and others that your posts are a great place to participate on social media.

Another great way to encourage engagement is to respond to comments. You need to engage with your audience. Thank them for their comment. If they pose a question back to you, answer it. Thoughtfully engage with your community.

One thing to avoid is wrestling with idiots. There are some people that love to fight. You could post, "It's a beautiful sunny day here in TN. I hope you have a great day," and someone will make a comment that you shouldn't brag about how great you have it when it just flooded in Louisiana three months ago. I get those type of comments. I even get some weird comments from people that jump on my post to slam me, the government, and other money sucking government contractors. I block those people pretty quickly.

Platforms

While LinkedIn is THE place to be for government contractors, YouTube and TikTok are also both good platforms. That said, I always recommend that people take their style into consideration when choosing their platforms. Yes, I recommend using more than one. However, I also suggest starting with just one. Your style will dictate where you should start.

For example, if you are a gifted writer, LinkedIn is going to be the place to build your base platform. If you love shooting short videos, I would lean toward YouTube shorts. If you like long form videos, YouTube is also a great place to start. If you are all about photos, you start on Instagram.

One of the things to understand is that each platform has a base context. If you don't understand the context and treat every platform the same, you are going to have a hard time getting traction. If you don't really understand social media, simply Google your style, the type of content you plan to post, and see what suggestions Google has for you.

Analytics

Every platform has some sort of analytics. YouTube is hands down the best when it comes to data collection.

What types of things are you looking for? How many connections, subscribers, or followers do you have? How quickly are these numbers growing? What topics are getting the most engagement? What topics aren't getting any engagement? If you are on YouTube, you can also see things like watch time, where your subscribers are coming from, when your viewers are watching, and audience demographics.

That said, initially, don't pay attention to the analytics. Give yourself three to six months to learn the platform. After that, you should be reviewing your analytics on a monthly or quarterly basis. You can learn a lot about what is working and what is not working by reviewing the data.

Advertising

I have mixed feelings about advertising on social media. Initially, I don't recommend it. It's often a complete waste of money because it's a lot like gambling in the beginning. This is one of the reasons that companies will often give you several hundred dollars in incentives to place your first ad. They are similar to casinos. They know that the suckers are the ones that don't understand how the platform works or how ads work.

The best ads are actually not ads. You read that correctly. The best ads are not actually paid ads. They are your best performing content (as proven by analytics) that you then run ads against. When you know something works, you tip the odds in your favor. This means your ads feel less like a blind hand of blackjack and more like you have x-ray vision that allows you to see the cards of everyone at the table before they are even played.

Create great content. Monitor the analytics. Only run ads against the stuff that takes off. That's the best formula for success with social media advertising.

Not Perfect. Prolific!

No one is perfect. Perfect is an unrealistic standard. Don't chase perfection. Be prolific! It's okay if you post something and only two people like it. It's okay if no one likes it. Keep posting! I promise you, if you are prolific on these platforms, you will start winning. I can't tell you when, but I can tell you from experience and with certainty, it's just a matter of time.

Everyone has a tipping point. We just don't know when it will come. If you follow the tips in this chapter, you will move closer to your tipping point much faster.

Chapter 10.
Intro to Value-Mapping™

Value-Mapping is a process developed by Joshua Frank. Some of you may remember it by its original name, competency-mapping. The end result of value-mapping will help you identify and clearly communicate your value in your marketing pieces (website, capability statement, briefings, etc.), proposals, and your 45-second pitch. It also helps you create several artifacts for your proposal library. The full process for this often takes two to three months of intense work. This chapter can't possibly do this topic justice, but it will introduce you to the concept and get you started.

In this chapter, I'm going to give you a scaled down version that you can run through in an afternoon. Refer to the full Value-Mapping process in Federal Access.

When I start working with a new client, I start this process by reviewing examples of a few corporate overviews with them. They are designed to help the client think about metrics, the value their company provides, their past performance, and the results they've achieved.

My initial goal is to make your marketing material communicate that you have actually done the work you say you can do. Most companies are focused on buzz words and jargon, yet don't communicate anything. You know what I'm talking about. We've all seen corporate overviews that use buzzwords like synergy, innovative, disruptive, cutting-edge, paradigm shift, next-generation, best-of-breed, best-in-class, and so on. When the average person reads these words, their first thought is not that you are a great company. They hear the voice of Charlie Brown's teacher "wah-wah-wah-wah."

Metrics and past performance communicate that you are more than capable of performing work on a contract because you've done it for other customers. The greater your metrics, the more you communicate your ability to scale your solutions.

You also need to understand that contracting officers review hundreds if not thousands of capability statements and websites each year. Most of them are bland and use the same jargon. And guess what? Most companies can't do the work. The moment that your marketing screams VALUE, you will separate yourself from the crowd and be taken seriously.

Corporate Overview Examples

LEAD Training has facilitated over 55,000 hours of executive leadership development for more than 16,000 students in over a dozen countries and all 50 states. We specialize in instructional design and have developed and deployed over 150 performance improvement solutions.

Vets2PM alumni manage more than $6.5 billion in project management portfolios annually for fortune 500 companies. With over 850 PMP certified graduates, Vets2PM is one of the nation's largest and fastest-growing PMP certification and placement companies in the country exclusively for veterans.

For more than 30 years, MSR Roofing has delivered roofing materials to more than 3,000 job-sites. We provide general contractors with "just-in-time" delivery using a fleet of 25 trucks and delivery systems.

Since 2008, Epcon Partners has facilitated the installation of 2,200+ miles of Natural Gas Liquid pipeline, 15+ compressor stations, 8+ facility expansions, and more than 500 successful projects for the oil and gas industry.

RSM Federal has been in the government contracting space for over 30 years. Our team of coaches have helped our clients win over $14.6 Billion in direct contract awards, trained more than 23,000 contractors, and have more than 2,500 members in our Federal Access coaching and training platform (Our delivery model). Our specialty is helping our clients master the art and science of government sales. We provide all of the strategies and tactics (the science) and show you how to actually apply that to your business (the art).

Since 2005, Meridian has been helping the worlds most recognized brands tackle complex enterprise digital transformations. Those brands include: Walmart, Coca-Cola, Blue Cross Blue Shield, Target, Home Depot, Lowe's, Tractor Supply, Office Depot, Office Max, and the Inspire food brands to name a few. We have a team of over 1,000 consultants deployed on-site with our clients to support over $984 Billion in annual revenue and more than five million employees. On average, we save our clients approximately 43% on project costs. This has helped our clients save over $23 Billion. Our primary differentiator is our people. We have invested nearly two decades building a database of 1.4 million vetted experts. The average company takes three to five months to find and place a purple squirrel. We can interview, vet, prep, and place one of our experts in three to five days. This includes cleared individuals at the TS/SCI level.

Your Corporate Overview

Now that you have an idea of what some sample overviews look like, let's talk about your company.

Gather a list of your top five contracts. Initially, it doesn't matter if those are commercial or government. We are trying to identify your metrics to eventually create what I call a roll-up of your numbers. More on that below. For now, let's deep-dive into your contracts. What did you do for the client? What results did you achieve? How many people or users did you serve? Are the users all in one spot or are they spread out all over the country or world? Did you increase anything or reduce anything?

In addition to the metrics mentioned in the examples above, here are a few more examples to help you think about your possible metrics.

- Successfully completed over 250 Oracle deployments
- Supporting more than 1.6 million users worldwide
- Deploying more than 35,000 cloud services via AWS annually
- Saved customers more than $100M in project costs
- Completed a 30% cost reduction in IT infrastructure projects
- 95% reduction in cybersecurity incidents
- Reduced downtime by 40%
- Maintained 99.99% uptime
- Reduced project development time by 25%
- Achieved a 98% on-time delivery for over 1M products per year

- Reduced help desk response time by 65%
- Maintained 96% employee retention rate across all contracts
- Innovative packaging solutions reduced shipping costs by 38%

When I start this process, I'm typically looking for big numbers and percentages here. However, if you are new, you might not have big numbers. That's okay. You have to start somewhere.

As you break-down your contracts, a common theme should emerge. What metrics are showing up on every contract? In an ideal situation, you will find two to three metrics. That's plenty for this round.

One of the first challenges you may encounter is that you can't find a common metric. This is often the case when your company does fifteen things. If your business model resembles this, take a step back. Focus only on the contracts that are your core competency. This will make sure you are comparing apples to apples and it will make it easier to spot these metrics.

If you still can't find similarities, maybe you have to think outside the box. How many projects have you completed? How many miles of cable were installed? If you are struggling to find a metric, get one of our coaches involved. If you're a member of our group coaching program, Federal Access Advisor, we have weekly live interactive sessions. If you're having challenges with value-mapping, you can bring it up during these sessions and we'll help you.

Once you have your metrics, it's time to write/update your corporate overview which will become part of your 45-second pitch; you will use it to update your capability statement; and these components are incorporated into your website and proposals.

ChatGPT Prompt

Here's a simple trick to write your corporate overview. Most people struggle to start this from scratch. It's often easier for a third-party to help with this since we aren't as close to it as you. However, there are also some shortcuts. My favorite trick is to use artificial intelligence (AI). I use ChatGPT for stuff like this all the time. Here's the prompt I would start with. This is what you type into ChatGPT:

Create a corporate overview for my company. We were founded in 2004. Our specialty is executive coaching. Our core metrics include: training more than 23,000 government contractors, helping our clients win more than $14.6 billion in government contracts, and serving over 2,500 clients. Please limit the overview to 100 words and do not use jargon.

Here's the output from ChatGPT with that prompt:

Since 2004, we've been leaders in executive coaching, helping government contractors succeed. We've trained over 23,000 professionals, supporting them in competitive environments. Our clients have won $14.6 billion in government contracts. With 2,500+ satisfied clients, we focus on practical leadership development and tangible results. We're dedicated to excellence and remain a trusted partner in shaping success for government contractors.

Here's the deal. This isn't perfect, BUT I wasn't expecting it to be perfect. I expected it to give me a foundation to work with and it did that. Massage it until you are happy and move on. Don't get bogged down by obsessing over every word. Now that you have a solid corporate overview, add it to your capability statement, website, sales pitch, bids, and proposals.

You're Not Done Yet

This completes my scaled down version of Value-Mapping. You could stop here; however, I would recommend continuing this process by going through your other contracts looking for similar data as well as anything you might have missed. Perhaps there's another metric that you can uncover. If you have a ton of contracts, analyze 5 to 10 a week until you go through them all. Keep adding to your original metrics.

How often should you update your marketing materials? You don't have to update your marketing materials every week or every month. My best advice is to look for metric milestones. You just crossed a million users? That's a significant update. Make the change. One of my goals during this process is that you see the value of incorporating value-tracking into your everyday life. This means that instead of occasionally breaking down your contracts, you are constantly keeping track of your metrics. If you do this, you will be able to update your marketing materials on regular basis.

Another benefit of walking through this process is that it should help your sales / business development team. For example, what if you discover that what you thought was your value, isn't? What if you discover that the main reason clients choose you is something that you aren't even talking about? Now you can arm your team with this information and they will do a better job communicating that to your customers. If you've been selling the wrong value prop for years, and you fix this, your sales should go through the roof.

Notice that I NEVER talked about socio-economic statuses in this chapter. Why? Because your status is not your value. Regardless of what some experts will tell you, your status is not the reason why the government is going to buy from you. It can and often will help **influence the acquisition strategy**, but your value, capabilities, and ultimately your ability to communicate all of this is why you will win a contract.

Chapter 11.
Nine Core Marketing Tools

There are nine core marketing tools that every government contractor needs. These tools will help you communicate professionalism, your value, and show that you are serious about being a government contractor. These tools are also designed to help you build your brand and position your company with teaming partners.

1. Capability Statement

The first one that I'm going to talk about is probably the most obvious. This is your capability statement. I did an entire podcast on this one. That podcast is episode 241. It's called *7 Elements of a Great Capability Statement*. It walks through this in detail for you. Most people know what's in a capability statement so I'm not going to get too deep into this one. Just understand there are seven key elements to it.

1. Corporate overview
2. Past performance
3. Areas of expertise or core competencies
4. Contract vehicles
5. Corporate data
6. Contact information
7. Certifications

2. Business Card

The second thing that you need is a business card. If you are in government contracting, what are you likely going to be doing? You are likely going to be attending conferences and events. You're likely going to be visiting customers. You're likely going to be visiting with teaming partners. Everyone is going to ask for your card.

I don't recommend anything too fancy. You'll probably change it from time to time. Don't invest in 10,000 business cards just because it's cheaper.

Just buy the bare minimum out of the gate. Use those, and then if you want to make any changes before your next order, you aren't stuck with boxes of cards.

The core items that need to be on your business card: your name, your company, your contact information, and a little bit about what your company does. Maybe a few of your NAICS. You just need to make sure that if your company name doesn't describe what you do, that you actually put some sort of description on the card.

I always recommend you leave some room on the back or on the side so that people can take notes. As a side note, two things YOU should write on cards anytime you get one: 1) Where you met and 2) What you talked about. This allows you to properly follow up after you meet someone.

I don't recommend glossy cards. However, if you want glossy, only get it on the front. Don't get glossy on the back. It's difficult to write on glossy cards.

3. Professional Email Domain

The third thing you need is a professional email domain. I can't tell you how often somebody emails me from a Yahoo, Gmail, or an Outlook email domain. I recently received an AOL email – I kid you not. These free generic email accounts are not professional. Obtaining a professional email, based on your corporate email domain is both simple and inexpensive.

There's absolutely no reason not to do it. You can get an email domain for between $20 and $100 a year. That's how cheap it is. You absolutely 100% need a professional email domain. All of those freebie email domains communicate that you can't afford a professional domain, don't care about it, or don't understand how to get one. All of those things scream amateur and raise unnecessary red flags about your company.

4. Signature Block

The fourth one is your signature block. Your signature block is a marketing tool. You should use it that way. Most people don't even put anything in their signature block. Not even their name. When they write an email, they might add their name or initials. You should use your signature block to communicate specific things about your company. I don't recommend that you put every award you've ever won, back to high school or second grade. That should not be in there. I've seen more than a dozen awards listed in some people's signature blocks.

I don't recommend that you have more than a couple links in your signature block. Make sure that you put https: - not just http. If you don't use the secure link URL, it will get your emails sent directly to spam most of the time.

If you're having problems hearing back from people and you've got a lot of links in your email signature, take a look at them to make sure they are secure. That could be a problem you didn't realize you had.

What do I recommend? I recommend your name, your contact information, your title, your company name, and a tag line if you have one.

In my situation, I'm part of four Amazon number one bestselling books. I have links to those books since they communicate that we're pretty awesome. It's always great to highlight cool things that you've done.

This is one of the few places where you can brag about yourself and your company. If you've written a book, won a major industry award, or hit a major milestone in your business, put that in your signature block. It communicates your success.

5. Your Website and Government Landing Page

The fifth one is your website and your government landing page. You need a website, that's number one, and you need a government landing page. I can't tell you how often I talk to a company and they don't have a working website. Your website should not take you more than a couple of days to stand up. In fact, I've purchased domains and setup templates in less than an hour.

Think small with your initial website. You only need three or four pages. Your main landing page, about us, contact us, and your government page. If you have that, the rest of it can take a few weeks or months. The core website pieces are the things that people are going to look at when they actually look up your company. You can also use a one-page website that covers all of these sections.

The reason you need a government page is that you want to stand out to the government that you are serious about this market. What should be on your government page? Keep it simple. It's just the information that's on your capability statement. That's all it is. It's just in text form on your government page. I also recommend that you have a PDF download of your capability statement, because not everybody wants to hit print on your page. And guess what? Sometimes pages on websites aren't printer friendly. You want to control what that printable version looks like. That's why you want a PDF download on your government page. Make it simple for them. Don't overcomplicate this.

I would also include testimonials and additional past performance information on your government page. This is a great place to expand on the limited information in your capability statement.

What if your company is solely focused on government contracting? Then it's likely that your entire website is government focused and you don't need a specific government page.

6. Capability Brief

The sixth tool that should be in your toolbox is a capability brief. If you are going to be talking to contracting officers and teaming partners, you're going to need a capabilities brief at some point. This is nothing more than an overview of your company. It's going to be 10 to 15 slides at most.

This brief is an overview of your company. It talks about your past performance and it covers key aspects of your capability statement. You should also include agency specific items. Anytime you present your capability brief, you *tailor it to that specific government prospect*. For example, if you are focusing on three contracts on an agency forecast, you should have a slide or two about those contracts. This communicates that you've done your research and it provides talking points to help you learn more about those opportunities.

Understand that you are going to slightly modify this each time you use it so that it's customized for the conversation. If I'm talking with the Air Force, I'm going to modify my briefing to highlight all the Air Force work that I've done. When I'm talking to the Army, I'm going to put all my Army work in the presentation. I may even modify my color scheme to match the agency or department.

7. Introduction and Capability Statement (ICS)

The seventh thing is something most people have not heard of. This is your introduction and capability statement. We call it the ICS. This is a tool that our clients use to impress teaming partners to get on teams.

We have a sample of the ICS in Federal Access. This document is usually around 15-pages. It's a PDF version of your capability brief along with your capability statement. It should also include specifics about the opportunity that you're trying to chase and how you can help this potential teaming partner leverage all of your skills and knowledge to make that teaming partner extremely competitive. Done properly, this document will separate you from all of the other subcontractors that are courting your preferred teaming partner.

8. Social Media

The eighth marketing piece is your social media. When it comes to social media in government contracting, you don't need much more than LinkedIn. You don't have to worry about Facebook, X, or any other tool; at least not initially.

You are going to use your LinkedIn account on a daily basis to connect with contracting officers, program managers, teaming partners, small business representatives, and many other players in the market. If you aren't sharp on LinkedIn, start with the basics. Learn the platform. Use the platform to post things about your company; to ask questions; produce polls about your industry; to network with other contractors, contracting officers, teaming partners; and to communicate with other experts in your field.

Initially, setting up your profile is probably the hardest part. You need a professional photo, a great headline that describes what you do (get this from your corporate overview), take portions of your resume and update your experience, and finally, use parts of your corporate overview for your About section. You should be able to get this setup and looking professional in one afternoon.

9. Book

The ninth and final marketing tool is something that not everybody has, but if you have this, this is like a nuclear marketing tool. It's one of the best things you can do. I rave about this all the time. *You should write a book.* If somebody walks in and they have a business card and a capability statement, and I walk in and I have my book and I'm an authority figure on a subject, who do you want to hire? At a minimum, you want to pick my brain.

Secretly, everybody on the planet that I've ever met wants to write a book. Your book will make you an instant hero.

There's nothing more powerful in marketing than writing a book. The really cool part is that it can open doors for you where nothing else will. And guess what? It's simple to market. Drop a book link in your signature block, put a linked photo of your book on your website, bring copies of your book with you to events.

Given the fact that the government has their $20 limit on gifts, make sure the price is under $20 so that you can give it out without breaking any rules.

Chapter 12.
Seven Key Elements of a Great Capability Statement

If you're a government contractor, you likely know that you need a capability statement. In the last chapter, I introduced you to the seven key elements that make up a great capability statement. This chapter is going to walk you through those key elements and how you can set up your capability statement to be a cut above everyone else.

1. Corporate Overview

The first section is your corporate overview. Your corporate overview should be one of the first things that someone reads. It should be three to five sentences. It should cover how many years you've been in business, your core metrics (as discussed in chapter 10: Intro to Value-Mapping, and it should be centered around your niche. It should also create a wow factor. When someone reads your overview, they should have no doubt that you can deliver on your promises.

The whole purpose of the corporate overview is to grab the attention of the contracting officer, program manager, or teaming partner and make them understand that you've not only been in business for a while, but that you can actually do what you say you can.

If you have not gone through the exercise in chapter 10 for creating your corporate overview, I suggest you flip back and review that section now.

2. Past Performance

Your past performance is number two. I like to highlight your three largest contracts. Use the logos of the agencies and the name of the contract IF it's recognizable. If it's not recognizable, don't use the contract name. Are you technically authorized to use logos? No, but everyone does it. If a client requests that you take them off, take them off. Most won't say anything.

One other tip on past performance. If you have a lot of contracts, customize this section of your capability statement based on who you are meeting with. For example, if you are meeting with the Air Force, be sure to have Air Force contracts on your capability statement. If you don't have Air Force contracts, any DoD contract will do.

This brings me to an overall capability statement strategy that you should be utilizing. When you're talking to a contracting officer, don't just give them your generic capability statement. After you're done with your conversation, customize your entire capability statement based on your conversation. Move things around to highlight that you listened during the conversation. This is an expert strategy that almost no one uses because most people tend to just have one capability statement.

3. Expertise, Core Competencies, Differentiators

The third section is your areas of expertise, core competencies, and differentiators. You don't need all three. This section is helpful in scenarios where your main NAICS code is very generic. For example, if your main NAICS is 5415111 – Custom Computer Programming Services, that likely doesn't describe the type of work you do. Use this section to expand on the type of programming you do, the key languages you focus on, and your core platforms.

4. Contract Vehicles

Number four is contract vehicles. As much as I like having this on a capability statement, I don't litter the whole page with them. Some companies collect contract vehicles like baseball cards. Just because you're on a vehicle, doesn't mean it matters to the CO you are talking to. Be selective about these. Focus on the big ones first and then agency specific ones for the agency you are briefing. Limit this section to between three and five vehicles. These include GSA multiple award schedules (GSA MAS), blanket purchase agreements (BPA), and other indefinite delivery contracts (IDC) / indefinite delivery indefinite quantity (IDIQ) contracts.

5. Key Corporate Data

Number five is your key corporate data. Your SAM Unique Entity Identifier (UEI), CAGE code, top five NAICS, and PSC codes. You don't necessarily have to put the descriptions of all your NAICS. Simply having the code is usually good enough. This section should not take up a ton of room, but it should be visible and highlight what you do. If you have twenty NAICS codes, list your top five.

6. Contact Information

Number six is your contact information: name, phone number, address, website, email address, and the name of your main point of contact.

7. Certifications

Number seven is your certifications. There are two types of certifications. Both are important. The first is your socio-economic certifications like SDVOSB, 8(a), WOSB, ISBEE, ANC, etc. You should have those logos on the page. Just don't do what most companies do and make them 25% of the document. Make them small, but noticeable. Remember, your certifications/status are not your value.

The second type of certification are industry and technical certifications. For example, many IT companies have Microsoft certifications, project management certifications, AWS certifications, etc. These are important and should be near your areas of expertise.

Bonus Section: Awards

The last thing I want to mention here is a bonus section. If your company has received special awards, you *might* want to include them. If it's not a significant award, I would not include it. Nobody cares that you won an award 20 years ago for small business of the year. What have you won recently? Agency specific awards are also great. If you were the Veteran business of the year for the DoD and you are prospecting with the Army, they are going to care about that award.

Chapter 13.
Sales Goals and Metrics

Government sales is NOT about finding things to bid on.

It's about finding opportunities you can WIN!

If you wanted to, you could find a dozen things to bid on every day. The problem is not a lack of opportunities in the market. If that were the case, there wouldn't be a thousand bid-matching services in the market.

This chapter is going to help you put metrics in place to track your sales goals. When I sit down and talk to a new client, one of the things they always tell me is, "my goal is to win more contracts." And while that is a goal, it's not a very clear goal. This chapter will help you add clarity to your goals.

Revenue

Most company goals start with revenue. What's your revenue goal? If you're a salesperson, what is the quota that you're trying to reach on a monthly, quarterly, or annual basis? The reason we start with revenue is because that is the foundation for all your economic goals. Once we have this goal, we can work backwards.

The first question you may ask is, "what's a reasonable revenue goal?" That depends on your resources. If you are a well-established company with dedicated salespeople, you are going to have a drastically different goal than someone who just launched their business and is operating more like a side-hustle.

I typically advise clients to focus on winning three to five contracts in their first year. You want a mix of subcontract and prime opportunities as discussed in previous chapters. If you are running your business full-time and you are in what I consider start-up mode, it's conceivable to have a combined revenue goal of sub/prime contracts of $500K. Simply use this as a baseline in year one. You might significantly under or over perform. That's okay. We just need a starting point to work backwards from.

Conversion Rate

The next goal you need to consider is your conversion rate (CR). If you have been responding to opportunities, you will be able to use historical data to determine what your conversion rate is from proposal submission to contract win. From there, set a goal to improve that rate. I typically suggest starting with a 10% to 20% improvement. For example, if your conversion rate is 20%, set a goal to increase it by 10% which would create a goal of 22%. It's not massive, but it's a great place to start and it will make a big difference when you combine this goal with the other goals.

This goal is extremely important when it comes to your pipeline. It will help determine how many opportunities you need in your pipeline in order to make sure that you are hitting your revenue goals.

Your conversion rate is also a great metric because it provides insight into your sales process. Assume for a moment that your conversion rate is really low; let's say 2%. This is an indicator that you are either responding to the wrong opportunities or your proposal responses have a lot of issues.

It doesn't make sense to keep filling your pipeline with a 2% conversion rate.

You need to identify and address the problems or you will waste a ton of time and energy chasing opportunities you can't or won't win.

If your conversion rate is 2%, your first goal is to get it to 10%. That's a 400% increase and it should be the bare minimum that you are trying to achieve with proposals. It's the difference between having to respond to 50 contracts to win one (2% conversion) versus responding to 10 contracts to win one (10% conversion).

Average Contract Value

Let's say that you want to hit a million dollars in revenue, and most of the contracts that you're putting in your pipeline are $50,000. If you have a 10% conversion rate, you have to put a lot of opportunities in your pipeline to hit a million dollars. In fact, you are going to need to put $10 million in your pipeline to ensure you hit your revenue goal. At 50K per opportunity, that's

200 opportunities. That's a lot of work. You can address this challenge by simply changing the average contract value (ACV).

If you increase your ACV to $250K, you only have to put 40 opportunities in your pipeline. That's an 80% reduction in the amount of work you have to do. Would you rather chase 200 or 40 opportunities? Now you understand why this metric is so important.

One of the things that I love about metrics is how a little bit of math can help you zero in on areas you need to improve and if used properly, these simple formulas can help you determine the best use of your resources. The best thing about metrics is that they don't lie. They don't hide anything. You can't ignore or hide from your metrics! Your strengths, weaknesses, and everything in between will be in black and white. Metrics aren't always fun to see, but they are extremely powerful. That's why you need to establish a solid set of metrics and track them.

Prime Versus Subcontracting

The next goal that you need to consider is your prime versus subcontracting goal. Our recommendation for companies *new to the government market* is to have a 70/30 split in your pipeline. You should be the subcontractor on 70% of the opportunities in your pipeline and prime for 30%. Remember, this is when you are new to the market. As you grow and gain past performance this metric is going to flip and you're going see yourself as the prime 70% of the time. You will still have 30% of your pipeline as subcontracting work. This means you have a healthy teaming strategy.

The question you probably have now is: "How do I determine which opportunities are prime and which ones should be subcontracting?" Great question! When you are first starting out, focus your prime opportunities based on the Simplified Acquisition Threshold (SAT is currently 250K). Stay below or close to that number. If you come across a contract that's larger than that, bring it to a teaming partner until you have enough past performance to be competitive. Don't complicate this. Just use SAT to filter your opportunities.

Profit Margin

It's not about how much you make, it's about how much you keep!

A lot of companies don't even consider this one. Most companies believe that winning is all that matters. It's not. I've seen companies win millions and go broke because they weren't focusing on profit. Your profit margin is why you're in business. If you don't focus on profit margin, one day you will realize you're running a non-profit because you're not making any money. A healthy profit margin is around 20% for services and 10% to 12% for products. If you go below 10%, you risk a lot of problems. You will be one mistake away from losing money at any given point.

Sales Activity Metrics

This next section is another layer of metrics that will help you achieve your goals. Whether you are a one-person army or have a sales team, you should be tracking your daily/weekly/monthly activities that contribute to your goals.

The first activity is the number of calls you make. How many calls are you making on a daily, weekly, monthly basis? Those calls can be to teaming partners, contracting officers, government program managers, small business offices, you name it. But there's a certain number of calls you need to be making every single week, especially when you just start your business. Conversations turn into opportunities. You are always one conversation away from putting a new opportunity in your pipeline, getting awarded a sole-source contract, or being asked to join a team.

The second activity is the number of emails you send. In addition to phone calls, how many emails are you sending to people? I never just call people. I ALWAYS follow-up a call with an email. It's another touchpoint in your sales process. The other thing that I like about emails is that you can send them quickly. They can work in the background while you are making your calls.

The third activity is capability briefs. Your initial goal should be one to three per quarter.

Your fourth activity is RFIs and RFPs. If you aren't bidding, you aren't winning. There's no way around this. All of the activity you do should lead to the submission of a bid or proposal. If it's not, you likely aren't doing the right things.

There's one metric that I feel I need to address simply because people confuse this metric with conversion rate. That metric is PWIN. Your PWIN is your Probability of Winning a specific contract. This is NOT your conversion rate. In fact, your PWIN is just a guess. Your conversion rate is a factual number based on your submissions.

Your PWIN is determined by several factors. Those factors should be built into your Bid / No Bid process. If you don't have a Bid / No Bid process, you're in luck!

 We have a Bid / No Bid process you can download. This process includes instructions, an example worksheet, and a template. You can find these documents in Federal Access.

Your Bid / No Bid process asks questions like: Do I have past performance? Do I know the customer? Do I have the right teaming partners? Do I have the right certifications? Do I have the right credentials? You put all of these into a Bid / No Bid process and based on your answers, the process will spit out a percentage chance of winning that contract. That's your PWIN.

Dashboard

My next recommendation is for you to setup a metric dashboard to track all of your data. Some CRMs have these features built in and require little setup. However, you may still want to track some of this manually. It doesn't matter how you track this information. It just matters that you DO track it.

At any given moment, you should be able to look at your dashboard and determine if you are doing enough of the right activities to hit your goals. You want to review this information on a weekly or monthly basis at the very least. This will allow you to adjust your activity during regular intervals instead of waiting until the end of the year to question why you missed the mark.

Chapter 14.
Seven Key Ways to Build Your Pipeline

This might be one of the most important chapters that you will read in any book when it comes to marketing. Understanding and identifying who buys what you sell is the foundation for every great marketing plan.

This is the most overlooked step in marketing. Why? Because most people take a brute force approach to sales and marketing. They respond blindly to RFPs, email blast every contracting officer they can find, and wind up wasting a ton of time chasing the wrong prospects. This is the number one reason people are frustrated with government sales. They think it's the government's fault that they aren't getting a response for their efforts, but it's actually their own fault for targeting the wrong people.

The only way to avoid this mistake is to do your homework. We started this process in chapter five by running searches in USASpending and SAM.gov. Now that you understand who buys what you sell, it's time to target your top three agencies and drill deep into their worlds. You need to become a private investigator that is obsessed about finding every detail you can about your top agencies.

1. Searching SAM for Active Opportunities

One of the things that I love about the USASpending.gov and SAM's Data Bank is how much data is at your fingertips. When it comes to DoD, these reports are often behind as much as 90-days for national security reasons. The downside is that these databank reports are historical. Meaning, they are focused on contracts that have been awarded in the past. How can that be a downside you ask? If you only focus on historical data, you are going to miss current (active) contracts. Think RFPs and RFQs that are currently on the street. The other thing that you won't find in the historical contract data are RFIs and Sources Sought. This is why I suggest running opportunity reports in SAM. This will help you build a more complete picture of who's buying what you sell.

You are looking for a couple of things in your search. The first is simply information. Contracting officer names, contact information, contract information, and tactical (short-term) opportunities.

Here's the deal. I want you to be as strategic as you can, but you also need to keep the lights on. Tactical opportunities may or may not be with your ideal agency. They may not even be for your flagship product or service, but they should be easier targets that you can win. Don't just look for multi-million-dollar tactical opportunities. Think smaller, such as simplified acquisition opportunities that are equal to or less than $250,000. These types of opportunities are great because they shouldn't require a lengthy proposal response or the normal amount (if any) past performance.

One of the main things you are going to look for are RFIs and Sources Sought. This is a pre-acquisition stage of the game that allows you to ghost your strengths and capabilities and start a dialogue with your agency. More on this in chapter 22.

2. Reviewing Forecasts

You can usually Google agency forecasts. Search [agency name, annual procurement forecast]. This is often how I find forecasts. However, it's not always that easy. Sometimes it doesn't matter how hard you search; you won't be able to find anything. This is a great opportunity to email a contracting officer or small business representative. Simply ask them for a link to their forecast. Let them know that you've been searching and can't seem to find it. This is usually an easy email to get a response to because it doesn't require a lot of work for the contracting officer. Also check Acquisition.gov's website for recurring agency procurement forecasts. You'll find them at https://www.acquisition.gov/procurement-forecasts.

Once you have the forecast, review it for opportunities that line up with your products and services. You often have to read between the lines on these because not all forecasts are complete or detailed. In fact, most aren't. But they do contain valuable information that will help you understand what's going on and being procured with your agency.

Let's assume for a minute that you are a cabling company that focuses on data cables. Think fiber, CAT 5/6, etc. You're reviewing an agency forecast and see an opportunity labeled "New HQ Building in GA." That opportunity will likely show up with a construction NAICS code. But guess what they are going to need when they build that building? Cable! You can instantly identify this as a possible opportunity where you can subcontract. Which means you need a solid teaming strategy to find a prime. Guess where you are going to find that prime? Two places. The first is in the SAM Data Bank. You should be able to look up that agency and run a report on construction NAICS. That will give you an initial list. The next thing I'm going to research is when the industry day is for this project. These types of projects often have full-day walkthroughs. Your potential teaming partner, your potential Prime contractor, is likely to be at that event.

Another way to use a forecast is as a tool to call contracting officers. Whether you see opportunities for your niche or not, when you call contracting officers, you want to be able to point back to their forecast. You will say things like, "Hi Susan, I was reviewing your forecast and had a quick question about ABC123 opportunity..." or "Hi Bob, I was doing my research and noticed that you had an RFI last year about ABC, but I don't see any RFPs scheduled for this year. Are you still working on this?"

3. Having a Solid Teaming Strategy

Regardless of where you are in your stage of growth, you need a solid teaming strategy. Why? Because, executed properly, you will put more opportunities in your pipeline, have more access to information about your prospects, and increase your chances of winning.

I discuss teaming in more detail in chapter 19. For now, just understand that it's important to work with other companies. Have you ever heard the phrase, "many hands make light work"? It takes a lot of work, energy, and time to win a government contract. Especially contracts of significant size. The more help you can get the easier this process becomes.

I look at teaming in four phases. The first phase is where you are dependent on other companies to help you get past performance. In this phase, you are almost always a subcontractor. In phase two, you have enough past performance where you can be the prime on smaller contracts. You will likely leverage the Mentor Protégé program as the Protégé in this phase. In phase three, you phase out of your small business status and rely on teaming partners to bring your company on their team as a sub for small business contracts while winning larger contracts. In phase four, you are large enough to compete with big primes for big contracts AND you become the Mentor in Mentor Protégé arrangements allowing you to leverage MP joint ventures.

4. Employees On Site

Are you getting information from your employees on a regular basis? And when I say regular basis, I mean daily, weekly, and monthly reports from them. They don't all have to write daily reports. But if something goes down in the office today, and it's a big deal, I want a phone call or an email. Don't wait until the end of the week or end of the month to shoot me a note and say, "Something major happened. Our primary email server crashed and the prime doesn't have a backup. We can fix this, but we need you to talk to the client." This is the kind of thing that should initiate a phone call.

The bigger picture here is that you need to be training employees to gather intelligence while they're on site.

Key personnel should notice the other contractors that are working on site. Who does the government like? Who do they not like? What problems are they talking about on a regular basis?

If you train your employees to listen for problems and look for opportunities, they should be your number one source of market information and intelligence. We have additional instructions on this process in the Value-Mapping resources within Federal Access.

5. Attending Events

The government has multiple types of events that you can attend. The one thing in common with most events is that there are typically influencers (contracting officers, small business reps, and program managers) in addition to potential teaming partners.

These people might be able to ignore an email or phone call, but it's really hard to ignore you at a conference or event. This makes events one of the few times and places that allow you to have meaningful conversations with key people.

The odds of you being awarded a contract at an event is probably less than 1%. However, you will likely learn about upcoming contracts that you can start gathering information on as well as position your company for capability briefings or other meetings with influencers. Meetings lead to opportunities.

There are typically six types of events that you will come across. Conferences, industry days, reverse industry days (pitch events), awards dinners, webinars, and matchmaking events.

How do you find events and determine which ones are a good fit for your company? There are three primary ways to find these. The first is networking. Talk to teaming partners, contracting officers, and colleagues. Ask them about the events they are attending. I guarantee you will learn about events you didn't know existed. The second way is Google. Perform searches on various phrases such as, "Your industry, government conferences and events," "your statuses, government conferences and events," and general phrases such as "government conferences and events." The third way is to check our lists. We have our top events listed in chapter 28.

6. When You Lose an RFP

When the average sales person loses an RFP, they move it to the lost column and forget about it. This is a mistake. At a minimum, you should use this failed attempt to get an informal debriefing with the contracting officer. More on informal debriefings in chapter 22. There are two other things you should consider when you lose an RFP.

The first thing to consider is putting the recompete on your calendar. If this is a multi-year contract with option years, you need to consider a recompete strategy. Since you have the time to properly prepare, you can put this on your calendar six to twelve months in advance and give it the attention that it deserves. This includes meeting with the contracting officer, program manager, teaming partners, and maybe the current prime. These types of meetings don't happen overnight. If you wait until the new RFP drops, you won't be prepared.

The second thing to consider is scheduling a capability briefing with the contracting officer. If the contracting officer executed one contract in your wheelhouse, they can and likely will execute more. You can use this briefing to gather information about other opportunities and position your company with that CO. More on requesting and running capability briefings in chapter 17.

7. Expiring Contracts

You can pull a list of expiring contracts from the SAM data bank. This is one of the most popular searches that new companies use. My primary recommendation is to look for contracts expiring over the next twelve to eighteen months. Small contracts under SAT won't require a ton of research and prep, but large ones will. This is why you will want up to eighteen months to gather information, talk to contracting officers, and form teaming relationships.

The odds are that you only need to run this report once per year, per product or service. Just remember that if you add new products or services or if you change your niche, you will want to run these reports again.

Chapter 15.
Managing Your Pipeline

Filling Your Pipeline

In the last chapter, I touched on ways to help you build or put opportunities into your pipeline. In this chapter, I will walk you through some of the nuances that will help you manage what you are putting into your pipeline and how to walk these opportunities through your pipeline effectively.

First off, understand that a healthy pipeline cures a lot of problems. The only time this isn't true is if your pricing is off and you aren't profitable. Otherwise, filling your pipeline is hands-down the most productive use of your time.

Filling your pipeline needs to be, at a minimum, a weekly habit. It's a lot like exercise. If you get out of shape, it's hard to reengage and when you start back up, it's because you've "accidentally" gained fifteen pounds and it's too late. If you stop filling your pipeline, you will wake up one day and your pipeline will be empty and it will take you a while to fill it back up.

Initially, you want your pipeline to have a tight filter. That filter is your top three agencies and your flagship product or service. That should be the makeup of your pipeline. But what if you can't find enough opportunities to hit your goals with that filter? Then expand it. Think of your filter like a knob on a water faucet. Keep turning the knob until it's just right.

The first thing I tend to relax is the agency filter. If that doesn't fill your pipeline, look at the product or service filter. Add one thing at a time until you get the right balance. Don't make the mistake of removing the filter altogether. This will create too many opportunities that you can't possibly track. Slowly relax the filter until you have what you need and then STOP!

Pipeline Ratios

The number one ratio that we teach our clients is the 1 to 5 ratio. This is the number of contract wins versus opportunities in your pipeline. Simply put, for every contract you want to win, you need a minimum of five opportunities in your pipeline. This equates to a 20% win or conversion rate.

Just remember that this is a starting point. If your win rate isn't 20%, this number won't help you hit your goals. If your win rate is just 10%, your ratio is going to be 1 to 10. This is one of the core reasons you NEED to track these metrics for as long as you are in business. Because guess what? Your ratio can change. If you relax your filter or don't follow your bid / no bid process, your win rate could decrease. If it does, you need to know as soon as possible.

Did you know there are different types of opportunities? If not, this section is going to help you understand some of these types and the ratios that you need to be putting into your pipeline.

The most obvious type of opportunity is determining whether it's a prime or subcontracting opportunity. This is fairly simple. Do you check all of the boxes by yourself or do you need a partner? If you are below 75% on your bid/no bid process, you shouldn't attempt to be the prime. At a minimum, you need to be a sub. Your ultimate goal is to get to a point in your business where 70% of your pipeline is prime opportunities, but many companies start with the reverse where 70% of their opportunities are subcontracting.

Remember this. Your goal is to WIN contracts. That's it. It doesn't matter if you are the prime, a sub, or even a second-tier sub. You want to win. These best practices are designed with winning in mind.

One of the challenges that I see with pipelines is that people tend to overload them with long-term opportunities. A long-term opportunity is any opportunity that is more than six months out. That's a long time. A lot can change in six months. It's very common for the government to extend an RFP by months or even years. That doesn't even account for pre-award and post-award protests. Some larger contracts may take two years to be awarded due to protests and then another six to twelve months before they start dropping task orders. This is why the majority of your pipeline opportunities need to be short term opportunities that are planning to drop in the next three to six months.

Assume for a moment that you are 100% going to win a big contract that is dropping nine months from now. You've talked to the CO and PM on the contract and there's no doubt that you are going to get this contract. What are you going to do for cash flow between now and when that contract is awarded? Unless you already have a healthy backlog of work, you will likely be eating Ramen Noodles for a couple of months. No matter how much you love Ramen Noodles, they get old after a few days. This is why it's important to not only look at the volume of what's in your pipeline, but also when these opportunities are dropping so you aren't caught in a cash slump.

Another type of opportunity that throws people off is direct awards versus indefinite delivery indefinite quantity (IDIQs). One of my first clients was a company that was brand new to government contracting. When I first met with them, they had about $150K in direct contracts and several IDIQs. They had spent their first year and half focused solely on contract vehicles. They were literally collecting them like baseball cards. They would win one and then put it in the trophy case. Then it was off to collect the next one.

Winning an IDIQ is just the first step. Once you win one, the real work begins. But this company was counting those IDIQs like I would count direct awards. It felt like money in the bank to them.

When you are just starting out, your focus should be on direct contracts. You win, you do the work, you get paid. This should be 90% of your pipeline. We advise that you only pursue one or two, maybe three contract vehicles per year. It depends on the size and complexity of the vehicle. More on contract vehicles in chapter 24.

Using a CRM

There are hundreds if not thousands of CRM tools in the market. As I write this, my favorite CRM is HubSpot. I love their free version. I've been using it for over five years. That doesn't mean I'm going to use it forever. I was an early adopter of Salesforce and Zoho. Both of those tools evolved over time and became too complex for me. I like simple tools. I don't need a bunch of bells and whistles.

There's a great video that shows you how to setup a new HubSpot account and build your opportunity stages. You will find this video in Federal Access.

There are five things that I want my CRM to accomplish: 1) Track opportunities by stage, 2) Manage contacts, 3) Run reports, 4) Track activities/notes for opportunities and companies, and 5) Manage a sales team. Most CRM tools can do 100 things beyond these five. Those tools are great, but they are above and beyond what you need.

All of these CRM fields are great, but I'd be remiss if I didn't highlight the activities/notes section and its importance. I've always had an incredible memory. In fact, my memory is so good, that I rarely take notes in a meeting. But there are two scenarios that my memory can't avoid. The first is my age. The older I get, the harder it is for me to remember things. Part of that is tied to the next one. As my business has scaled, I've gone from working with 5 to 10 clients at a time to having hundreds of clients and thousands of connections. The top ones are fairly easy to remember, but there's no way for me to keep track of everything these days. It's just too much information.

The other downfall of not keeping notes is when you are working with a team. Without notes, your team is going to wind up doing double the work without taking advantage of the important information that you've collected.

Taking notes will fix this problem. They allow your team to review information and activities before placing a call. This prevents you from wasting time reviewing an opportunity that you've already reviewed, or making some other costly mistake.

Pipeline Stages

One of the most important parts of your CRM are pipeline stages. Again, I tend to keep this simple. These stages should mirror your sales process. I like the following stages because I think every opportunity can fit into one of them. However, you will likely modify and maybe even expand these stages over time. Most companies do.

1. **Pre-Acquisition:** I put RFIs, Sources Sought, and opportunities that I'm talking to COs about that aren't in the active acquisition stage in this bucket.

2. **Identify Strategy:** Use this stage for multiple things. This is when you are going to run your bid / no bid process, think through your teaming strategy, and ultimately decide if you

are going to advance this opportunity to the next stage, defer it to another round, or simply not bid on it.

3. **RFP:** The RFP stage is pretty self-explanatory. At this point, you've submitted a proposal and you are waiting on a decision.

4. **Recurring Revenue:** I like using a stage like this for multi-year contracts so that you can track recurring revenue easily.

5. **Closed Won:** This is usually a default stage in your CRM. This simply tracks what contracts you've won. This stage will be very helpful in determining your win rate.

6. **Closed Lost:** This is usually a default stage in your CRM. This simply tracks what bids you've lost. This stage will also be very helpful in determining your win rate.

As you grow, you will likely expand to between 7 and 10 stages. For example, some companies like to have two stages for RFPs. One stage for working on the proposal and one stage once it's submitted and has moved into source selection. That's fine. You may even add other stages. My advice is to start simple and expand as you spot a need.

I want to be very clear about something. It doesn't matter to me HOW you track all of this information. It's just important that you DO track it. It doesn't matter if you use a CRM, a Word document, or an Excel spreadsheet. Track this information so you can make informed decisions. You will thank me later.

Moving Opportunities Through Your Pipeline

The key question you need to ask yourself about an opportunity in your pipeline is: *What's next with this opportunity?* The answer to that question is often one of the following:

- I need to reach out to the CO and ask about the status
- I need to try and ghost a capability
- I need to assemble my team
- I need to respond to an RFI or RFP
- I need some past performance to be ready for this RFP

- Hire a proposal or capture manager
- I need to schedule a capability brief
- Perform a pricing analysis
- Establish a relationship with a supplier
- Run a competitor analysis
- Prep my proposal team
- Get a certification

This is a short list of some of the things you may need to do to move an opportunity to the next stage. It's not an exhaustive list, but it's a good start.

One thing to keep in mind is that some of these items aren't simple. For example, it may take you fifteen phone calls and a dozen emails to schedule a capability briefing. Getting a certification may take weeks or months. Running a competitor price analysis could require hiring an outside consultant until you learn how to do it yourself.

This is another reason that we use stages and focus on moving opportunities through the stages. The stages help keep us on track and moving forward.

Weekly Pipeline Reviews

When I first start working with a client, one of my questions is: How often do you review your pipeline? The answer is usually: "what pipeline?" We both chuckle and then start building their pipeline. After your pipeline is built, I advise having weekly pipeline reviews with your team.

The main focus of your pipeline review is going through each opportunity, in each stage, and asking three simple questions:

1. What's next with this opportunity?
2. Should we be chasing this?
3. How can I help you?

These three questions will help ensure that opportunities don't become stagnant in your pipeline. Stagnant opportunities often lead to an inflated pipeline that provides a false sense of hope.

If you are a solopreneur, you still need to have this pipeline review every week. The only thing that changes is question three. Instead of asking how you can help, you should be asking, "what help or questions do I have for my coach?"

If you follow this simple process, you should walk away from your pipeline reviews with a clear set of action items each week. As you progress through your weekly reviews, you should be following up on action items and working with your team to navigate the challenges that come with each item.

A good example of this is scheduling a capability briefing. Assume that you are trying to schedule a briefing and can't get in touch with a CO. Bring that up in your pipeline review or with your coach. The next step with the opportunity remains getting a capability briefing, BUT part of your review is brainstorming ideas with your team on HOW to do this. Maybe you are asking too many questions. Maybe you've moved away from your script and there's something obviously wrong with it. Maybe you've only called twice and need to keep calling. Reviewing your activities with your team is often a simple way for an aha moment that could lead you to accomplishing your tasks and moving an opportunity to the next stage.

Chapter 16.
Six Ways to Reach Contracting Officers

This is probably one of the top five questions that I'm asked by government contractors. How can I reach contracting officers? This is a struggle for many reasons. The primary reason is that contracting officers are overworked. The average contracting officer receives over 200 emails per day. They can't possibly respond to all those emails. That's just their emails. They also receive countless calls and voicemails per day. If all they did was respond to emails and calls, they would never accomplish their primary job of managing contracts through the acquisition process.

This chapter discusses six ways that can help you reach a contracting officer. The first couple are a little obvious, but I want to talk about some nuances that should help these strategies be more effective. One of those nuances is that it's really important for you to actually do your homework. If nothing else, you need to come prepared with specific questions so you don't waste anyone's time.

1. Phone

Let's dive in and talk about the most obvious way to reach a contracting officer. The first one is the phone. The challenge for a lot of folks is that you're going to get voicemail a large portion of the time. What are you going to leave in that voicemail?

If you leave a 10-minute message in your voicemail, *you are not getting a call back*. If you over-introduce yourself, you're not getting a call back. If you try to give your entire 45-second pitch, you're not getting a call back.

When I call somebody and leave a message, I simply say something along the lines of, "Hey Barbara, this is Michael. I had a really quick question for you about (insert contract name). When you get a chance, please give me a call back. Here's my number. I'll shoot you a follow up email. If it's easier for you to answer via email, that's perfectly fine. Thank you." It takes about 15 seconds to listen to that voicemail. Given the fact that people can see how long each voicemail is, do you think a contracting officer will listen to your one-minute voicemail or my 15-second voicemail first? Probably mine. Which means yours might not even get listened to.

You might get somebody to answer the phone, you might not. If they don't answer on the first try, guess what you should do? Call again. I call people as many as 20 times over a reasonable period of time (two weeks) *before I leave my first voicemail*. But I don't stop there. I keep calling until I get an answer. The average person will typically call two or three times before they give up. Don't be that person. Keep calling. Don't leave a message every time. If you do, you will start to feel like a stalker.

2. Email

Email is one of my favorite methods for reaching anyone. I love this method because I've worked really hard at writing emails that get responses. My emails are similar to my voicemails. Very quick and to the point. I'm not trying to do a whole capability brief over the phone or via an email. I'm just trying to get the answer to a specific question and then start a dialogue with that person. If you've sent 3, 4, 5, 6 emails, and you are not getting a response, I highly recommend you copy the small business representative or another influencer on your emails. That simple addition may make someone respond to your question quickly.

3. OSDBU or OSBP

The Office of Small Disadvantaged Business Utilization (OSDBU / federal agencies) and the Office of Small Business Programs (OSBP / Department of Defense) are designed to advocate for small businesses to ensure that they have opportunities to win government contracts.

To find the right office, simply Google OSDBU or OSBP and the name of the agency or military command you're trying to work with. Because of their advocacy role, these offices have quite a bit of influence in the market. When they reach out, contracting officers tend to respond.

If you are having an issue reaching a contracting officer, reach out to the OSDBU or OSBP and ask for an introduction. While you're at it, ask them if you can also give them a capability briefing. They may also know other contracting officers who buy what you sell and be willing to introduce you.

4. LinkedIn

There are millions of government employees and contractors on LinkedIn and that number is growing every day. You likely already have a LinkedIn profile. You just need to use it to connect with folks and start conversations. In fact, I recommend that before you call or email a contracting officer, try to connect with them on LinkedIn. Invest a week going through their profile learning about them. Like, share, and comment on their posts. If you do this for a week or two prior to calling them, you won't be a stranger when you call. You will be their colleague from LinkedIn.

5. Organizations

There are thousands of great organizations that focus on advocating for small business and specific industries. Some of my favorite organizations are the HUBZone Council, Society of American Military Engineers (SAME), the National Veteran Small Business Coalition (NVSBC), National 8(a), and the Armed Forces Communications & Electronics Association (AFCEA). All of these organizations have conferences and events. The leadership of these organizations are passionate about helping their members. They do this through meeting with leaders at agencies, lobbying congress, and working to make the contracting landscape a better place for everyone.

These organizations will bend over backwards to connect you with small business reps, teaming partners, and experts that can help you with any challenge you may face.

I highly recommend that you find and join the organizations that best fit your socio-economic status and industry. Go to their conferences, volunteer to be on their committees, and get to know the movers and shakers.

I should warn you to start small. Pick one or two organizations to join. It's better to pick one organization and build deep relationships than it is to join a dozen and not have the time to devote to them.

6. Snail Mail

The last one is going to be way outside the box for some people (some of you may be surprised to learn it even still exists). It's worked for me in the past. There's a lot of variations to it, but it's a fun one and its snail mail. Today we don't get a lot of stuff through the regular mail. If you send an oversized postcard or a really nice wedding invitation to somebody, they're going to open it.

Your mail could simply be an invitation to connect with you for a meeting. It could also be something really creative like a full-size poster of your capability statement. Imagine getting a poster in the mail. That kind of effort would at least make you chuckle and notice that business. It might impress you that they went to that length to reach you. That's all it takes to get noticed and cut through the clutter of inboxes and voicemail.

If you use this strategy, be sure to follow-up via phone and email. In fact, all of these strategies work best when you use all of them together. The magic you are looking for is in the follow-up and the variety of ways you reach out.

Chapter 17.
Capability Briefings

One of your primary goals for reaching out to contracting officers, small business representatives, and program managers is to schedule a capability briefing. You will use this tool to introduce an agency to your business, ask questions about upcoming opportunities, create opportunities, and gather intelligence that you will use later to land teaming partners.

What Goes on Your Slides?

- Your corporate overview
- Leadership overview (key personnel only)
- Your primary NAICS as well as product/service descriptions
- Differentiators
- Past performance examples
- Client list/logos
- Awards and Certifications
- Contact information
- Questions about their forecast or upcoming contracts
- No more than 10 slides

Should you Bring Your Capability Statement or Not?

The short answer is no. A lot of people in this industry will advise you to bring a generic copy of your capability statement to every meeting, conferences, etc. This is bad advice for one key reason. You can't possibly build a generic capability statement that will be perfect for every situation. It's impossible.

You should plan on customizing a version of your capability statement after every meeting. Why? You want to highlight key points from your conversation in the document. This is the best way to make a great impression on anyone you speak to.

Running the Meeting

Plan on talking about your company for about ten minutes. Any more than that and your prospect is going to start tuning you out. People don't want to hear you talk about yourself. They want to talk about their organization and their challenges.

After you've gone through your core slides, you need to spend the rest of the meeting asking questions. Your focus should be on learning more about their organization, upcoming opportunities, and challenges that you may be able to address.

Questions to Ask

- I'm curious if you already have an acquisition strategy in mind for this opportunity? For example, do you already have a contract vehicle in place that you would like to use?

- Are you planning to go with a set-aside category or full and open?

- I noticed on your forecast that this was planned for the fall, is that still the case? If so, when do you think the RFP will come out?

- Will there be any pre-acquisition activity on this such as an RFI, sources sought, or an informational webinar? (This depends on the size of the opportunity. If it's tiny, they probably won't do this, but if it's a complicated acquisition, they might.)

- I'm curious, why now? What is driving this acquisition now?

- Is it possible for you to introduce me to the program manager?

- This kind of work is right up our alley. Do you know of any other opportunities similar to this that we should be aware of that weren't on your forecast?

- Does this fall under SCA pricing?

- Do you happen to know the previous contract number?

- Who's the end-user? Which command, etc.

- Will this be coming out on SAM or another site?

- Does your organization participate in industry days, events, or conferences where I can meet you and your team?

- Based on what we sell, is there a colleague of yours that I should connect with?

- We are looking to team with a few companies. Can you recommend a couple of contractors to us?

- How do you do this today?

- Are you using a specific method, procedure, or process for this?

- We completed a similar project for one of our other customers. Would it be helpful for you if we arranged a meeting with our PM who led that effort? You could pick their brain on lessons learned.

How Often Should You Request a Capability Briefing?

Did you know that your current clients are 27 times more likely to buy from you than a new prospect? There have been countless research studies backing up this statistic. The main reason this has stood the test of time is because people buy from people they know, like, and trust.

If you perform well on a contract, you will quickly gain trust with your clients. People are simple creatures of habit that like doing business with the same companies for years. As long as you maintain that trust, you should be able go back to your customers repeatedly. The good news about gaining trust is that you also gain access to your customer. Meaning, if you call or email, you get a response.

I recommend reaching out to your clients every six months to request a capability brief. One reason is to stay on their radar. Another reason is to introduce them to new product or service lines as well as other important updates. The most important reason is to gain face time and collect market intelligence. For example, if you just landed a new contract vehicle that will make it easier for your client to purchase from you, that's an important update. Also consider things such as socio-economic certifications, figuring out a solution for one of their key challenges, or forming a new joint venture.

On-Demand Capability Briefings

What do you do when you're having trouble reaching a contracting officer? The obvious answer is you just keep trying to reach them. You keep calling and emailing until you get through. That's one route. You could also try to get creative.

I would create an on-demand version of your capability brief. I recommend you keep it to 10 minutes or less. If you really want to spice it up, create a foundational capability brief video. That video is something that you use over and over. When you send it out, create a custom 30-second message for the contracting officer that you're sending it to.

Also consider using a tool like Loom. When your prospect clicks to watch the video, you will get a notification. This lets you know when you should reach back out to them.

Once you have this video, you can also share it on social media and put it on your website.

Chapter 18.
Seven Tips for Writing Better Emails

The average office worker receives 121 emails per day. Contracting officers (CO) can receive double that. How do you stand-out in a crowd of over 200 emails? More important, how do you get a response? The short answer is that you need to level-up your email game. You need to get better at writing compelling and descriptive subject lines, expressing gratitude in advance, leveraging LinkedIn, and much more.

1. Do Your Homework

Number one on my list is do your homework. It's probably the simplest one that you can do. All you have to do is a little bit of research on the person you're reaching out to. It doesn't take a lot of time to scan SAM.gov, USASpending, their LinkedIn profile, and the organization's website *before you reach out.*

While there technically aren't any stupid questions, if you ask an obvious question that could have been answered in 10 seconds on their website, you are going to leave a bad impression. The CO is going to look at your email and immediately know you didn't do your homework. This is irritating. This may cause them to ignore your email.

One of the things that I do to preface the fact that I've actually done my homework is start an email by literally saying, "I've been doing my homework and have a couple of questions about...." Now you've set the tone that you've not only done your homework, but that you aren't going to waste their time. They will appreciate that and this could be the reason you get a reply back.

2. Name Drop

This is probably one of my favorite tips. Name drop if possible. It may look like this, "Hi Susan, I've been talking to Bob Smith (she should know that name) and he suggested that I reach out to you about…"

If you can name drop someone that they likely know, the odds shoot up they are going to respond to your email. If you copy that person on the email, the odds are very high that they will respond.

My favorite name to drop is a small business representative.

3. Limit Your Questions

Limit your questions to just two or three; perhaps only one. If you send an email, even with the best questions in the world and you ask seven to ten questions, you probably won't get a response. Asking a ton of questions is like assigning homework. Contracting officers don't have time for this and they won't have time for you if you write them a novel.

Some contracting officers might have really good intentions and want to respond to your email, but they will also realize that it's going to take 30 to 45 minutes to respond to you. In this situation, they will plan on doing it later. But, later never comes. They find fifty other things to do and you never get a response.

4. Simple Questions

Someone recently emailed me and said, "I have two quick questions for you." When I started looking at the questions, they were correct. They only had two questions. However, each question had multiple sub questions. They were labeled A, B, C, D, E, etc. In total, they had really asked about 15 questions. But, that's not all. None of their questions were simple or specific. Almost every question they asked was based on vague scenarios and required follow-up questions for me to gain clarity. How quickly do you think they received a response? It took me a couple of days because of the complexity of their email. This individual was a client so I had to answer them. I'm compelled to. A CO doesn't have the same compulsion. Make your questions simple and direct.

5. Descriptive Subject Lines

I can't tell you how often I get an email and it simply says "question for you," or "question," or something along those lines. If I am sifting through 30, 50, or 100 emails and I just have one that says "question," I'm skipping it. It's human nature to scan your emails to see if anything jumps out. If something does, that's the email you're going to respond to first.

For example, if your subject line reads, "Would you consider extending the Q&A period?" That's the kind of subject line that would grab my attention. It piques my interest and I probably know that I can respond to that email quickly.

Half the battle is getting someone to open your email.

If they open it, a lot of times they're engaged, they're invested, and they want to deal with it. This is why the subject line is important when you're writing an email.

6. Thank Them in Advance

Here's a simple example, "Hey Susan, I really appreciate you taking a look at my email. Thank you in advance for any help or direction that you can provide on this."

You're dealing with government employees in a relatively thankless job where they're constantly getting pounded about one thing or another. Not everybody's going to care that you wrote "Thanks in advance," or "I appreciate you," but some will. Some may even look at it and think, "Sure you do. Why should I believe you or care?" But there's going to be a handful, maybe even more than that, who are going to see it and think, "I like the tone of this email. I like the way they wrote that. I appreciate it. I'm going to respond to this person simply because they were nice to me."

This isn't hard to do and it's one more tool in your tool bag that will hopefully allow somebody to read it and respond to your question.

7. Update your Subject Lines

When I was working with the Tony Robbins team, one of the things that they were adamant about was updating the subject line of emails if the subject changed. If it was a brand-new subject that had nothing to do with the previous email, you had to start a new email with a brand-new subject line. That was just the way they did business. They wanted the subject line to be descriptive of what the topic was about and they didn't want long email chains that constantly changed subjects.

I can't tell you how often I will get an email from someone that I haven't talked to in one, two, or even three years, and it's a reply to an old email that has absolutely nothing to do with the email chain we originally started years ago. For contracting officers (for anyone), that is irritating. If you have a new subject or a brand-new topic that has nothing to do with the last one, start a brand-new email chain with its own subject line.

Chapter 19.
Teaming With Other Companies

One of my favorite growth strategies is teaming. It doesn't matter whether you are a start-up with no revenue or a billion-dollar company. Teaming, done properly, will add a significant number of winnable opportunities to your pipeline each year.

When you are getting started in government contracting, 60% to 70% of the opportunities in your pipeline should be teaming opportunities where you are the subcontractor. This isn't just for past performance reasons. You learn a lot from teaming. For instance, if you are a subcontractor on a team, you will learn the proposal process without having to do the heavy lifting.

There are other things you can learn from teaming such as pricing, processes, which conferences to attend, who the important players are at your target agencies, and even get introductions. A good teaming partner wants to help you because they understand the value of having a good teaming partner.

The challenge with teaming is that it takes time and effort. You need to find the right teaming partners and take the time to build trust with them. This doesn't happen overnight.

Your Strategy

A great teaming strategy starts by clearly defining who you are looking for. If you have identified your target agencies, this process gets a lot easier. If you haven't done this yet, I highly advise doing this before moving on.

Once you have your top agency identified, start looking at who is currently selling to that agency. Those companies should be at the top of your teaming list because they are *already selling to your agency*.

The next step is your teaming stable. You are going to hear this phrase a lot. Your teaming stable should be comprised of multiple size and status companies. Initially, your stable should include one of each of the following: 8(a), WOSB, SDVOSB, HUBZone, and one large prime. If you are selling to an agency that often uses Indian Small Business Economic Enterprise (ISBEE), Native Hawaiian Organization (NHO), Alaska Native Corporations (ANC), or another status, you should include those groups as well. Once you have one of each category, your next goal is to add more companies to your teaming stable. Ideally, you will have at least two from each category. However, you may have more than that depending on your top agencies. In fact, you may have a completely different set of teaming partners for each of your top agencies.

Two of the main goals of teaming are to increase your chances of winning and to gain past performance. While those are important goals, the other major goal is to increase the *number of opportunities that your partners bring to you*. These are what I consider inbound leads.

Inbound leads don't just happen. Initially, you have to prompt your partners. How do you do this? You lead by example. You should be bringing opportunities to your partners on a regular basis. Quarterly at a minimum. This not only shows your willingness to team, but that you are putting in the work.

Don't just bring your partners opportunities that they have to prime. As you gain past performance, include your partners on opportunities where you plan to prime. This strategy is really powerful in situations where you don't need a partner. If you could win a contract by yourself, your partner will realize that. You don't have to spell it out for them. Give them one or two FTE's. This shows your commitment to working together.

If you don't have an opportunity every quarter, at a minimum, schedule a meeting with your partners. It's easy for companies to get busy and forget about each other. A simple update meeting can often lead to your company being added to a team.

How do You Convince a Prime to Put You On Their Team?

A prime will want you on their team for one key reason. Your ability to give them a competitive edge that ultimately makes them more likely to win a contract. That competitive edge comes in many forms. Some of the most common reasons include: information you have gathered on a contract, a relationship you have developed with an agency or key personnel, a contract vehicle that you are on, a status that you have that they don't, a similar status that allows them to meet the minimum prime percentage of performance on a contract (think similarly situated entities), a unique product or service offering, a special skillset, or your relationship with other teaming partners.

All of these are great reasons to put you on their team. But there's one reason that will get you work over and over again. The reason is that you've worked together enough that they know, like, and trust you. You become their lucky pair of socks. Have you ever heard of a ball player that wears the same pair of socks because they feel they are lucky? A lot of us do this. Whether it's a tradition before or after a win or wearing a special set of socks or shirt, many people feel comfort in having their lucky charm with them.

I'll admit that I have a lucky charm. I always wear my Iron Man socks when I speak at an event or when I attend an awards dinner. There's something about those socks that makes me believe we are going to win or that I'm going to knock it out of the park. And guess what? We've won every award when I wear those socks. Be your teaming partner's pair of lucky socks.

Prioritizing Your Potential Teaming Partner List

What if you don't yet have a stable of teaming partners? Or, what if your stable doesn't provide a solid choice for an upcoming opportunity? Once you identify a potential contract you want to chase, the next thing you should do is pull a report in SAM to create a list of potential teaming partners who are already selling to that agency. Once you have a list, narrow it down to ten or less companies to research. At this point, you want to find some simple ways to prioritize your list.

When I'm prioritizing a list of potential teaming partners, I start by looking at the opportunity first. How large is the opportunity? What type of past performance is it going to require? Is it going to come out via a specific socio-economic status? Will the contract require a clearance? Will the contract require a specific contract vehicle? Is proximity to the place of performance going to be part of the evaluation criteria? These are all considerations that will help you prioritize.

An example might look like this: While speaking to a contracting officer, you learn they are planning to put an opportunity out in the fall that is around

$10M. This opportunity is with NASA at the Johnson Space Center in Houston. All of the work will be done on-site. The government is looking to make this an 8(a) set-aside under the NASA SEWP contract.

If that's all the information you have, you have enough information to filter your teaming partner list. In this situation, you are looking for a teaming partner located in the Houston area that is 8(a) and already on NASA SEWP. Ideally, you are looking for a company that has a couple of contracts in the $5M to $7M range or slightly higher. Anything lower than that and you will risk that company not having relevant (contract value) past performance. Prioritize your potential teaming partner list based on these factors.

The last thing I do to prioritize companies is some quick research on their website. Does their website look professional? Is their leadership team listed on the website? Do they have a download of their capability statement that I can review? Is their contact information listed on the website? Can I easily find them on LinkedIn?

There's no right or wrong way to rank what you find online. However, you will likely get a gut feel based on their online presence. That gut feeling is all you need to determine who to call first and how to rank the rest of the list. Don't overcomplicate this. Just start reaching out.

Your Pitch to Teaming Partners

Your pitch to a potential teaming partner is actually very simple if you've done the previous steps. I would start with a call. Here's a simple script you can use:

"Hi Steve, this is Michael LeJeune with RSM Federal. I've been talking with Jan White over at NASA JSC about the $10M network upgrade contract that they are planning for this fall. I think we are in a unique position that would make your team extremely competitive. I was wondering if you would like to talk about teaming on this?"

Who's going to say no to that pitch? If nothing else, Steve is going to want to speak to you to learn what you know. Ideally, you should put a teaming agreement in place before getting deep into that conversation. However, you could talk at a high level before putting a teaming agreement in place.

Now it's rinse and repeat time. Gather intel and reach out to other teaming partners.

Another Strategy for New Contractors

There's a great video called "How to Find Teaming Partners for Subcontracting Work." This video is located in Federal Access.

I highly recommend this strategy for new contractors that are looking to self-perform on a contract. This is especially ideal for new companies where the founder is still working a job and doesn't have a ton of time for business development and writing bids or proposals. This strategy will help you replace your job with a contract. This strategy is best for service-based companies, but can work for product companies. It depends on the products.

The gist of this strategy is that you are going to run a report every month on recently awarded contracts for your primary service. You are looking for contracts that require multiple FTEs. These are likely 7 or 8-figure contracts. The opportunity may require a unique skillset.

You should be able to easily identify thirty of these contracts every month. That's one per day that you can engage and qualify. Reach out to the prime with this script:

"Hi John, Congratulations on winning the software development contract for the VA last month. If you are like everyone else right now, you might be struggling to hire one or two of those FTEs. If so, I'd love to talk to you about this. I believe I can help you.

Additionally, there are a couple of smaller contracts with the VA that we are targeting for the fall. If nothing else, I'd love to speak with you about teaming with us on one or two of those."

I guarantee you that this strategy will get you some meetings. It's a bit of a numbers game. Staffing is a major issue right now and it's not getting any better anytime soon. Whether there is a spot for you on the current contract or not, you need to be having these type of teaming meetings. The prime might have all the positions covered on their new contract, but maybe someone on another contract is leaving in the next three months and they don't have a replacement yet. You will never know unless you reach out and start talking to people.

Chapter 20.
Eight Ways Primes Evaluate Subcontractors

Do you struggle to get prime contractors to call you back? If you do, this chapter will walk through eight ways that they evaluate your company and how you can use this knowledge to your advantage. This is the key to not only getting a callback but also getting on the team of your choice.

I think this chapter is going to be eye-opening for you to understand why prime contractors don't call you back. The other thing that happens regularly is that you will have a great meeting with a prime contractor and after the meeting, they don't return your emails or calls. It's baffling. Why? The short answer is that every call, email, or meeting is a job interview. Whether you realize it or not, you are being evaluated.

1. Will You Make Them Competitive?

The first way you are being evaluated is probably the most important. The primary thing that primes look for is if you will make them competitive. If the answer is no, *the prime won't likely tell you to your face*. Their actions will speak louder than words. They will simply ignore you.

There are a lot of factors that go into making a prime competitive. At the end of the day, if you have not communicated how you are going to make them competitive, you have missed the mark and likely will not get a call back.

When you are working with a prime or trying to work with a prime, you should clearly use the words, "*Here is how we are going to make our team, including you, extremely competitive on this opportunity.*" The rest of the sections in this chapter are how you communicate that you will make them competitive.

2. Do You Know the Customer?

The first thing they're looking for is if you know the customer. If you know the customer, you likely have intelligence on the opportunity. Those are two different things, but they go hand in hand. If you don't know the customer, you likely don't have any intelligence on the opportunity. The prime is looking for you to say things like: "We have been talking to the contracting officer at the agency." "The reason that I think they're going to put this out WOSB is…" "I was talking to my contact at the agency and I learned that they are not happy with the current prime. In fact, they want to go a different direction on multiple contracts that this prime has."

Whatever it may be, you have to bring something to the table to let the prime know you've actually been speaking to that organization. It may be you haven't yet spoken to the government, but instead used to work at this organization with the program manager and have in-depth knowledge of how the organization works as well as relationships with key personnel.

3. Do You Have Past Performance?

Knowing people at an agency is great. Having past performance makes you even more valuable. If you don't have past performance, that doesn't mean you will be overlooked, but when it comes to choosing a team, past performance will definitely give you an edge.

Assume for a minute that you don't have past performance. What do you bring to the table in that situation? Instead of asking the prime to be on their team, you might focus on asking them to be on your team. The right scenario for this could be that you have a socio-economic status that they don't and only your company can bid on a contract. Whether you can do the work alone or not, this could be a strategic decision to ask the prime to be your sub. This is a great way to kick off your new relationship.

4. Do You Have a Unique Skillset?

What skills do you bring to the table? Are your skills complimentary or competitive with the prime? If you're both trying to do the exact same work, the prime isn't likely to want to share that work. However, if the skillset you have is hard to source, they might be short an FTE or two and don't want to risk or have the time to find those extra employees. Part of this is basic business acumen. You need to present your skills in a way where they don't come across as a threat to the prime.

In an ideal world, your skillset is unique and fills a gap that the prime has. For example, let's say you know about a large network installation that an agency is doing for a new building. The prime you want to work with has a great team for installing all the hardware, cabling, and setup of the system. But most of their engineers are level two and this contract requires two level-three cyber security engineers that they don't have. Your focus should be on those two level-three engineers if you have them. In this situation, you are filling a gap with a highly technical position that is going to be hard to source.

5. Is Your Company Mature?

Does your website look like it was built in the 90's? Does your capability statement look like a third grader drew it with a crayon? Do you sound like you know what you're talking about or do you come across as completely clueless?

When you meet a prime, they are not only looking you up and down and judging you. They are listening to your words. Are you on time for the meeting? If it's virtual, do you have problems with the technology? How do you act in the meeting? Are you professional? Do you follow-up and follow through with your promises?

Either before or after you meet, the prime is going to do an informal background check on you. They are going to look at your website, your capability statement, your SAM profile, your LinkedIn profile, and anything else they can get their hands on. Why? Because they are doing their due diligence to determine if you are mature personally and professionally.

Any of these factors could be a red flag to a prime. You've got to show a level of maturity and professionalism that makes them want to work with you and your company.

6. What Status Boxes Do You Check?

This is number six on this list. Why am I just now mentioning your socio-economic status? Depending on the type of contract, your status may not be a factor. Just because you have a bunch of check marks and statuses doesn't mean it's relevant to that opportunity. Your status will open doors, but it's RARELY the differentiator that makes a prime want to work with you. Why is that? There are two reasons. The first is that your status isn't unique. You're not the only company that does what you do, that has your status. The second reason is tied to the first one. A good prime is very likely to already have a teaming partner with your status, that does what you do.

When does your status come into play? Prime contractors have subcontracting goals. On occasion, the prime is short on their goals for some reason or another. Depending on their needs, your status might help them meet their goals. The other situation that is more likely is when the prime is evaluating partners to chase a contract vehicle. In that situation, your status is the first thing they check before wasting any time evaluating the other factors because the right status is required to bid on the contract.

7. Do They Have a Partner Like You?

If the prime already has a partner with similar skills, you need to make sure you differentiate your company in some way. The other criteria on this list become even more important in this situation. Do you know the customer? Do you have past performance? How deep is your skillset? Are we going to be competing for the same work? Do you have intelligence on the opportunity? And one of my favorites, did YOU bring them an opportunity first? If none of their other teaming partners brought them a specific opportunity, that alone could give you an edge and it could make the prime question those other partners. All of these factors come into play when you get down to the differentiation between you and the other companies courting that prime.

8. Your Relationships

What relationships do you have outside of this one opportunity? If I'm talking with a Prime and I start painting a picture of how we can work together on other contracts because of my network, that is going to factor into their decision-making process. For example, if I know they just lost a contract at an agency where I have contracts, that might be the carrot I dangle in front of them. No one likes to lose and everyone wants a shot at redemption. Maybe my company can help with that. This could be the thing that tips the scale in my favor on the initial contract I brought to them.

Here's a tip that you need to highlight. *Every conversation you have might be your last.* You need one or two things up your sleeve for every meeting. Notice I said one or two and not fifteen. Meetings are a precious luxury that should never be squandered. If you go into a meeting with nothing up your sleeve and with a singular focus, you are bound to be disappointed. However, what if there was a way to never be disappointed?

Let me run a scenario by you. Let's say you know a large prime is chasing a contract that you would be perfect for. You check all the boxes. You know the customer; you have intelligence on the opportunity; you have past performance; you have a unique skillset; and you even check all the status boxes. You show up to the meeting with the prime, go through your slides, and impress the hell out of them. You are on cloud nine because they are laughing at all of your jokes, shaking their head in agreement at everything you say, and smiling the whole time.

When it comes time to talk about a teaming agreement, the temperature in the room drops about fifteen degrees and they get very serious. They say something along the lines of, "I really like you and your company, but we just met with one of our teaming partners yesterday and signed an agreement with them. I don't think it's going to work to have you on this team. Maybe next time." If you don't have a plan B or C in your pocket, all you can do is thank them for the meeting and slink out of the meeting.

Here's what I suggest. Instead of slinking out of the room. Acknowledge the situation they are in and say this. "I completely understand. Would you do me a favor? Would it be ok for me to follow up with you on this contract if you win to see if the team needs an FTE or two? If your team gets into a bind, we might be able to help." They are going to say yes to this. Once they say yes to that, make your next move.

"While I have you here, I was curious if you have this other opportunity on your radar?" The plan here is they might not have this on their radar because it's something that you've been talking to your customer about that isn't on the street yet. This is where you ask them if they would be open to teaming on that contract. They will likely say yes. You've now kept the relationship alive and you're not slinking out of the meeting. Instead, you get to leave the meeting with a working relationship with your new teaming partner. Let's back up, this was your original goal. Sure, you came in with a specific contract in mind, but that wasn't the actual goal. The goal was to build a relationship with this prime so you could chase work together and your plan B accomplished that.

Chapter 21.
RFIs and Sources Sought

What's the Purpose?

The first thing to know is that Requests for Information (RFIs) and Sources Sought are *pre-acquisition* activities. This means they are part of the government's market research phase. They will likely be released weeks or months prior to an acquisition. This is a way for contracting officers to gather information from potential vendors and to see if anyone is interested in the work.

The responses to an RFI or Sources Sought helps the government determine how to proceed. This means that, when used properly to ghost your strengths and capabilities, they have an enormous amount of influence over how the government writes the RFP or if they just skip the RFP process and make an award.

How are They Different?

The main difference between the two is that a Sources Sought tends to be further along in the acquisition process. Note that I said "tends to be." That's not always the case, but in my experience a Sources Sought usually indicates that the government is very close to buying. The government often issues an RFP after the Sources Sought, but not always. A Sources Sought may feel a bit more structured like an RFP where an RFI might be a one-page list of questions that's less structured.

The key difference between the two is that Sources Sought are specifically designed to identify if the small business community is capable and interested in an opportunity. This is one of the primary reasons we encourage clients to respond to Sources Sought. If the government doesn't receive any responses, they may opt to cancel any further action on the opportunity or they may put it out for bid as full and open. This means that large companies will likely bid on it and that small companies will lose their competitiveness.

On the flipside, RFIs are for every company size and will result in both small and large companies responding. The purpose is typically to ascertain if there is a solution to a problem. Again, if no one responds, the government may cancel the opportunity.

How Time Intensive Are They?

As with everything in life, it depends. I've seen RFIs on a one-page Word document with six questions and I've seen some that are twenty pages. Product RFIs are often fairly simple. You can typically knock out a product RFI in a couple of hours. If you've responded to a few product RFIs, you can probably trim that time down to under an hour. Service RFIs might be a little more time intensive. It depends on how much background information the government provides and the level of detail they want in your response.

In general, an RFI or Sources Sought should not be time intensive after you've written a few. You should develop artifacts along the way to build up your proposal library. This will allow you to quickly respond to these types of requests.

What is the Timeline for Responding?

While writing this chapter, I went to SAM and set the search criteria for Sources Sought. The shortest due date was five days after the Sources Sought was published. The longest due date was six weeks after the published date. The average was between seven and ten days.

Why is there such a short window to respond? The main reason is that these responses shouldn't take a ton of time. You aren't writing a 300-page proposal. Your response might be six paragraphs. The other reason is that this is just one step in the acquisition process for research purposes. It's not a binding contract.

What if you miss the response date? Glad you asked. This is one of the major differences between this phase of the acquisition process and the RFP stage. You can typically still respond and the contracting officer will still review it. I suggest reaching out to the CO and asking them if they would accept a late response since you just found the RFI or sources sought. Whether they respond or not, you should plan on responding.

I can't tell you how many times a CO has told me that they put out an RFI and either didn't get a single response or only received one. They want responses to these and will often ignore the deadline to get a response. I'll take that one step further. I can't tell you how often a client has told me that they submitted a late RFI response and a few months later were awarded a contract based on that late RFI response. When they spoke to the CO after the award, the CO said they were the only company that responded.

How do You Use Them?

There are two things that you use an RFI for. The first is to strategically get on an agencies radar. This is a great way to introduce your company to a new agency. You have to follow-up on these. Use them to open a door and then walk through it by setting up a capability briefing.

The next is probably the most important. You need to ghost your capabilities and strengths. If you've never heard of ghosting, I'm going to give you a quick overview.

Ghosting is a process that we teach our clients to help them position their strengths and expose the weaknesses of their competitors to the government. You can do this in an RFP response, your capability statement, your website, and your capability briefings. One of the most important places to use this strategy is in RFIs and sources sought to influence the acquisition.

The goal of ghosting is for your competitor to look at an RFP and say, "Damn! This looks like it was written for my competitor." If you do this right, your key phrases, capabilities, and strengths will show up in the final RFP and make it hard for your competition to respond because they simply don't check all the boxes that you do.

How These Often Work

One thing is fairly consistent. That thing is silence. Sometimes it's a month and sometimes it's eighteen months before the government does anything. Then out of the blue, you get one or even three sole source awards.

In 2023, I had three clients win a total of eleven sole source awards based on RFI responses in a 30-day period worth more than $8 million. These were all one-to-three-page responses. All of them but two had almost zero discussions before making the awards. In two of the cases, the government called the contractor and asked them a ton of questions. It felt a bit like an interrogation. Then silence for a couple of months before the awards.

Another scenario that happens frequently is that the government will award a different contract that is unrelated to the RFI. I know how that sounds, but it happens all the time. When you ask about the original RFI, they say they are still working on it, but this one took priority.

A more common scenario is that instead of awarding a sole source contract, the government moves into formal acquisition and issues an RFP. This might be a month or even two years after the RFI is issued. It just depends on the complexity and priority of the need.

The final scenario is that the government determines, based on the responses, or lack of responses, that industry isn't interested in this type of work and they cancel any further activity on the RFI. Priorities often shift with the government and something as simple as a change in the White House may also cancel an RFI due to budget shifts. The point is that just because the government issues an RFI doesn't mean they are going to award a contract.

Chapter 22.
The RFP Process

When I speak to new contractors, without fail, every one of them asks me for tips about the RFP process. My biggest tip is that they need to understand the process. Once you understand how RFPs work, then you can work on the nuances of perfecting your responses.

This chapter is going to help you understand the big picture of the RFP process in three simple phases: before you respond, during the response period, and after submission. Each section will review what's happening as well as tips and tactics during those phases.

Before

Bid / No Bid Process: *Just because you can doesn't mean you should.* That's an important life lesson not just an RFP lesson. In the context of RFPs, just because you can bid on something doesn't mean you should. In fact, your bid / no bid process should be finely tuned so that you are primarily bidding on opportunities where the chance of winning is high. If I had to put a percentage on it, I would say the PWIN should be above 75% at a minimum. I would prefer that it's closer to 85% or 90%.

There is one notable exception. If you are new to the market and need some experience, find an RFP that is just right for your company and go through the motions. You will learn a lot from reading through an RFP and navigating your response to each section.

Other than this exception, there aren't a lot of good reasons to submit a low PWIN proposal. Proposals take a lot of time and resources. Don't go below 50%.

We touched on your bid / no bid process in an earlier chapter. However, this is so important that I want to remind you of a few questions. After all, this process helps determine if you are going to bid or pass (no bid) on an opportunity. Your bid / no bid process should be asking questions like:

- Is this the first time we heard about this or have we been tracking it?
- Do I have relevant past performance?
- Do I know the customer?
- Is the customer in my top three agencies?
- Is our pricing competitive?
- Do we understand the requirements?
- Do I have the right teaming partners?
- Do I have the right certifications?
- Do I have the right credentials?
- Do I have the right statuses?
- Do we meet all the compliance requirements?
- Do I have the employees or a recruiting system to get them?
- Do I have the cash flow for this?
- Is this opportunity too big for us right now?
- Do we have enough points to be competitive?
- Do we have the time to properly respond?
- Is this opportunity a must-win for us?

One thing to understand about your bid / no bid process is that it's not written in stone. It's meant to be used as a guide. If you answer no to a question, that doesn't mean you can't bid. It just means that you've identified an area that you need to mitigate in some way. Failure to mitigate increases your likelihood of losing the bid. Please don't ignore your weaknesses.

The Q&A Period: The Q&A period is one of my favorite stages of an RFP because it's one of the rare opportunities to significantly influence the requirements. When an RFP is released, there is almost always a Q&A period. That period might be three days or two weeks. During this time, you can submit questions to the government. Understand upfront that the government rarely answers your questions to your satisfaction. They typically compile all questions into a single document and then post the response to SAM after the Q&A period ends.

The problem with this process is that the clock on the RFP keeps ticking even if one of the questions during Q&A asks for an extension. For example, let's say that you are chasing an RFP that is due in 30-days and the Q&A period is 14 days. By the time you get the answers to the Q&A, you likely only have a week left before the RFP is due, if that. This means you can't wait for the answers to begin work on your RFP response, especially if you are facing a 200-page proposal. This can be extremely frustrating, especially in situations where the answer to your questions could cause you to no bid the opportunity.

This means if you have enough yeses to the bid / no bid process, you often have to gamble and start the proposal process on your end so that you can adjust-fire once you get the answers. However, I have a little trick that I've used to get an answer to my questions BEFORE the Q&A period ends. It's the language I use in my questions. Here's an example.

*"Hi Steve, we've been tracking the ABC opportunity for about six months and noticed that **the requirements changed between the pre-RFP last month and this version that came out today**. The main thing that I would like to bring to your attention is the addition of a facility clearance. This is a new requirement that we feel would **limit competition**. Given the nature of the work, this seems **unduly restrictive**.*

Would you consider either removing this requirement, sponsoring the winning company for a facility clearance, or extend the RFP due date by 60-days to allow every company tracking this opportunity to shift their strategy?"

There are three things that I want to bring to your attention. 1) I made it clear to the CO that we've been tracking this and the requirements changed at the last minute, 2) This could limit competition, and 3) This is unduly restrictive. All of these are lawyer speak for: buckle up Steve! You are setting yourself up for a protest. No one wants this.

This isn't just an example I thought up. I actually submitted this request to a CO on behalf of a client. Take a wild guess how long it took the CO to respond? I bet you're thinking they didn't. Well, you would be wrong. They actually changed the RFP within two hours of me sending the email.

The update to the RFP downgraded the requirement for a facility clearance upon award and the agency agreed to sponsor the winning company. This was a double win for our client who would go on to be selected as one of the winners on the acquisition.

Pre-Award Protests: Are you aware that companies can protest an RFP before it's even awarded? It happens, not as often as post-award protests, but it still happens. I see more of this on large multi-billion-dollar contracts. For example, in FY23, there were more than 350 protests to the National Institute of Health's (NIH) CIO-SP4 contract. That's hilarious and frustrating at the same time.

Should the protest tool be in your tool bag? Maybe. I'm not a fan of protests. Even if you "win," you may not win. I have one client that loves to pre and post award protest. I should mention that he is an attorney who happens to own a product company. In 2022, he won every protest he filed. Guess how many contracts he won based on those protests? If you guessed zero, you would be correct.

One of his worst protests was a pre-award protest. I won't get into the details of his protest, but I will say two things. The first is that he won the protest. The second is that the protest received a bit of media attention. As a result, instead of awarding to my client, the government started the process all over again and reissued the RFP. A competitor discovered this opportunity, bid on the reissued RFP, and they beat my client. The worst part is that this competitor would have never known about the opportunity if my client had just kept their mouth shut. This introduced an entirely new problem (a competitor) into the equation.

I'll say this one more time. Winning a protest doesn't put money in your pocket. You can win the protest and lose the bid. You can also tick off the agency, but that's a topic for another day.

Read the Whole RFP: For the love of chicken nuggets, please read the whole RFP before you make a decision to respond. DON'T wait until there's a week left before the RFP is due. "Come on Mike, people don't do this. It's so obviously stupid that this can't be common."

You have no idea how often this happens.

Here's a fun story. A client reached out to me five days before an RFP was due and said, "Mike, we have a problem. We are the incumbent on a $1.2M contract. This was our first contract and we haven't won't anything else so we don't have any other past performance. **We just noticed in the RFP** that the agency wants three past performance examples. What do we do?"

My immediate reaction was, "they either don't like you or that was a template and they forgot to remove it." You see, if an agency doesn't like an incumbent, they will purposefully put a requirement in the RFP that they know the incumbent can't meet in order to remove them from the contract. Through our discussions, I found that the government actually loved my client. This meant that the past performance requirement was likely a mistake. We reached out to the CO and brought this to their attention. *They removed the requirement* from the RFP and my client went on to win the recompete.

Here's the thing. The CO didn't have to remove this. They could have been embarrassed by the mistake or pushed back and said that this should have been brought up during the Q&A period. My client was wrong for not reading and noticing this immediately. Could they have protested? Maybe, but the odds of winning that protest were slim and it would have likely damaged their relationship with the agency.

Reading the whole RFP is not just about finding mistakes like this. You need to make sure you understand the requirements and can check all the boxes. If you wait until page 180 of a 200-page RFP to notice a requirement that you can't meet, you have likely wasted countless hours of your precious time and resources...and possibly lost an existing contract.

Please take time to read the entire RFP before you respond.

During

Proposal Prep: Once you have read the RFP and decided to respond, you need to prep for the proposal. If this is your first RFP, you may or may not have any resources or artifacts. That's okay. You are going to build these as you go.

If the RFP is fairly small, you likely don't need any special software or need to take a class on color teams. Are color teams and processes important? Yes. You can learn a lot from all of the formal proposal training systems on the market. However, when you are getting started in this business, you just need to get organized. I would argue that going through the motions once or twice will better prepare you for formal training. The experience of walking through a proposal will help you understand the training and help you ask better questions down the road.

If the RFP is 200 pages, requiring a complex response, and you have multiple writers, it might help to have some software in place. However, you can manage this with a simple process.

Regardless of the size of the RFP, there are two things you need to organize: People and Resources. I recommend that you start with a proposal kick-off meeting. This is where you bring your people together to review the proposal and assign responsibilities.

At a high level, you have five key phases of writing your proposal.

1. **Initial Review and Planning** – This is where you review the proposal with your team to ensure you are going to be compliant and if you have any gaps. You make a plan for mitigating the gaps and then make a plan to execute. This includes resource planning of people, tools, and processes.

2. **Writing** – Most of your time is spent writing the sections.

3. **Review and Revision** – Ideally, you want one main reviewer who can ensure that the proposal flows smoothly from section to section and has one clear voice.

4. **Compliance Check** – Once you are done with revisions, I recommend a final pass to ensure full compliance with all of the requirements.

5. **Submission** – The last thing you need to ensure is that the proposal is submitted *ahead* of the deadline. There are a hundred things that can happen that could interfere with your proposal submission. Don't let an internet crash or someone on vacation stop you from uploading your documents before the deadline. The government doesn't care about your excuses.

Build a Compliance Matrix: One of the best things you can do during your proposal prep is to build a compliance matrix. In fact, you can start this while reading the RFP. I know a lot of people that print out the RFP and use highlighters to mark every important requirement. You're looking for every statement that says the contractor "will," "shall," or "must" do something. This not only includes product and service requirements, but also FAR clauses. This ensures that you bring these items up to your team during the review.

Your reviewer(s) will use the compliance matrix during the compliance check process. My recommendation is to update this matrix as the proposal is written to include the page numbers of the proposal where each item is addressed. This will allow your reviewer to quickly jump to those pages and check for full compliance.

 We have an example compliance matrix in Federal Access along with a few proposal examples. These examples are great for understanding how to build your own.

Follow the Instructions: The easiest way to get your proposal disqualified is to not follow instructions. If the proposal has a page limit, you better be under that limit. Otherwise, you are non-compliant and you will be immediately removed from competition. Some proposals have more requirements than a college term paper. I've seen font size, font type, heading, footer, margin, and other requirements that have nothing to do with the content of your RFP. People tend to overlook these or just ignore them because they aren't paying attention to the details. Don't make this mistake.

If the proposal says the government is only accepting responses via email, snail mail, or upload to a website, that's how you submit your proposal. Proposal instructions are not there as a warning. They aren't yellow lights that you can ignore. Think of proposal instructions like the out of bound lines on a football field or basketball court. Stay in them.

Unlike an RFI, you also have to respond to *everything* in the RFP. A lack of a response is non-compliance. Non-compliance gets you booted from the process. Respond to everything in the RFP.

Key Sections of a Proposal

Government RFPs are widely known for following a similar process when it comes to their structure and sections. As serendipity would have it, the week before I wrote this chapter, I reviewed a dozen RFPs in just about every industry you can think of. The one common factor across all of them is that none were structured the same.

I'm telling you this to emphasize the fact that just because you don't see a section B or M in an RFP, doesn't mean that the information you are looking for isn't included. I'm also telling you this so that you don't just search RFPs by section B or M. If you are searching an RFP for pricing, instructions, SOW, etc., simply use those search terms in addition to section B, M, etc.

Here are a few of the most common sections you will write as part of your bid or proposal:

- **Executive Summary** – This is a bit like a cover letter. This is likely the first thing that the reviewers are going to read. It should give a brief overview of what you are going to cover, some history on your company, and some past performance that ties to the opportunity.

- **Past Performance** – Each RFP has a specific section for past performance examples. They ask about the agency, dollar value/size of the contract, a description of the work performed, contact information for the customer, and a few other items. This is an area for you to brag about your work. Use metrics and clear outcomes instead of buzzwords.

- **Resumes** – If this is a service contract with FTEs, you will likely be required to submit resumes for key personnel. Don't just upload copies of your employees resumes. Use a standard template. This is an opportunity for you to communicate that your company is professional and mature.

- **Statement of Work (SOW) / Technical Response** – Your technical response is a result of reviewing the requirements in the SOW and writing to each requirement. You don't want to simply restate, verbatim, what the government has written in the SOW and then answer it. You want to label your responses the same as the government's sections. For example, if the government says that section 1.5 is about network requirements, your proposal will have a section 1.5 and it will be about network requirements. DON'T create your own labeling system that doesn't mirror the RFP. That only creates confusion and makes it hard for the reviewers to know if you covered everything.

- **Pricing** – This is often submitted as a separate volume to your proposal package. This might be the hardest part of the proposal. This is often created in an Excel spreadsheet. It's going to have a comprehensive breakdown of how you arrived at your pricing. The government requires transparency in your pricing. This section is where you provide that. Also, expect the government to negotiate with you on your pricing. You don't have to budge, but when the government comes back and asks for your best and final offer, you either need to justify your price or lower it.

- **Terms and Conditions** – Often referred to as T&Cs, the terms and conditions are basically the contract terms that you are reviewing and signing.

- **Capability Statement** – One of the last things that you are going to attach is your capability statement. I've said this a few times now, but it bears repeating. Do NOT give them a generic version of your capability statement. This version of your capability statement should be customized for this opportunity and highlight everything that makes your company the perfect choice for this contract.

Negotiations: Once your proposal has been submitted, the government will go through their review process. This process is called "source-selection." This could take days, weeks, or even months. If the government is considering your proposal, at some point in the process they will likely reach out to you to negotiate your price.

Most companies fold here and give an extra percent off. You don't have to do that. You can simply come back with justification of your pricing. However, in an effort to be more competitive, you may decide to sharpen your pencil and shave a few points off your pricing.

This process could be as simple as one round of discussions and submission or it could go back and forth until an agreement is reached.

After

Agency Debriefings: Whether you win or lose the contract, you should ask for a debriefing. You need to do this immediately after you are notified of a win or loss. If you are requesting a formal debriefing, which I don't suggest, you typically have three days to request this.

Here's the problem with a formal debriefing. It requires paperwork and has risk. While the government loves paperwork, they don't like it when YOU are the one causing them to fill it out.

There are situations where you might consider a formal debriefing. The main situation is that you believe something shady took place during the evaluation process and you intend to protest. In that situation, you are trying to document as much as possible by having the government go through a formal debrief.

The other factor that most people don't consider when requesting a formal debrief is that the contracting officer has full authority on how they execute this and how much information they give you. If you ask for a debrief, a CO could send you an email that basically says, "We received over two dozen submissions. While your proposal met all of the requirements, your pricing was 20% higher than the proposal we chose and for that reason, you weren't picked." End of debrief.

That information doesn't really help you. That is why we suggest that you request an informal debrief. Use those exact words. Anything other than that is a formal debrief.

I recommend starting with a call and then following up with an email. Your call should sound like this:

"Hi Steve, would it be possible to just get an informal debrief? We want to build a long-term relationship with your agency and it would really help us to understand what we did right and what we did wrong in our response. Do you have 10 minutes to discuss? Nothing formal. I won't send an email. Just some informal questions to help educate me."

You will be blown away by some of the responses you get. Some people will say no and just tell you that you were overpriced. It doesn't hurt to ask. If they say no, then request a formal debriefing within three days of the formal notification that you lost.

One of my clients was recently denied their informal debrief. However, in the CO's response, she wrote him a bullet list of fifteen things they either did wrong or failed to communicate. He sent me the list and was devastated. I remember calling him excited. My response to him was that he should be excited too. He now had a detailed list of everything he needed to fix for EVERY proposal (not just that agency). And sure enough, he fixed the issues and won his next proposal with the same contracting officer.

Internal Debriefing: Your team can't get better if you don't review your actions. This means reviewing your wins and losses. What did you do right? What did you do wrong? Where did the proposal process fail? Did you have an issue with software or resources? Did you learn that Rob doesn't have the attention to detail to write a technical response?

These are all great questions to ask your team. My favorite question to ask is: How are we going to improve for next time? Let your team brainstorm some ideas. Some will be feasible and some will not be feasible. You might not be able to hire a full-time proposal writer just yet, but you can identify this as a future goal. The key is fostering an environment where the team is comfortable talking about all of this and brainstorming solutions.

Your internal debriefing is not a gripe session where you point fingers at each other. Talk about your mistakes but don't dwell on them and don't complain for the entire session. Make it clear upfront that the goal of the session is to get better, not beat each other up.

Award Notices: If you win a contract, you will be notified. The government normally has you sign off on the contract and then you move into the kick-off phase.

If you lose a contract, you will also receive notification. Win or lose, you receive notification. Are there situations when you don't receive notice of loss? Yes, but this doesn't happen often. This is why you review SAM daily to see if there are updates to the opportunity, such as an award being made.

If you are considering a protest, you typically have three days after the award to take action. For this reason alone, you need to keep checking SAM for the award. But, the three days don't begin until the government notifies you. If you look at SAM and the award was made a week ago, you email the contracting officer and request a formal notice that you lost. This will then initiate the three days.

Chapter 23.
SAP and Micro Purchases

I need to start this chapter by saying that I didn't want to write it. The reason I didn't want to write it is tied to its popularity on social media. Similar to the middleman strategy, "experts" tend to promote this as a magical solution to winning government contracts.

It's not.

Simplified Acquisition Procedures (SAP) and micro purchases CAN make it easy for a government buyer to buy from you; but you still have to do the hard work of calling potential customers, learning about their needs, building relationships, and packaging your solutions in a way that make these viable as acquisition options.

SAP and micro purchases are acquisition strategies. That means the buyer has already made the decision to buy. Think of it this way. If you want to buy a car, you will go through a decision process with a handful of questions. What kind of car do I want? What kind of car do I need? What features do I want? Will I buy a new or used car? All of those questions are part of your pre-acquisition strategy for buying a car.

Those questions will eventually lead you to a price range. Once you get to your price range, you will start honing your acquisition strategy. Are you going to need to look at dealerships or are you going to look on websites and social media for individual sellers? Part of that depends on your budget. Are you going to finance with the dealership or do you have cash? It all depends on the price of the car. What if you plan on using cash and a dealership offers you an amazing no money down and zero percent interest rate finance option?

Your options become more limited as the price of the car increases. However, when the price of the car is lower, you have a lot more flexibility. Even if cash is an option, you may choose financing because you prefer that option. It's the same with the government and contracting officers. Just because they CAN use SAP or micro purchasing doesn't mean they will.

I interviewed my friend William Randolph on this topic in episode 291 of our podcast Game Changers for Government Contractors. William is a micro purchase expert. William said that he reviewed his business at the four-year mark and noticed something interesting. There was a massive spike in revenue in month 30. It took him that long to build relationships and learn about his customers. Month 30 was his tipping point. This isn't magic. It's a science that requires a lot of hard work, repetition, and time.

Overview of SAP

Here's a quick overview of Simplified Acquisition Procedures. SAP is covered in the Federal Acquisition Regulation (FAR) in Subpart 13. SAP was designed to help streamline purchasing for goods and services that fall under the Simplified Acquisition Threshold (SAT). The SAT is currently $250K.

As long as the dollar value is under $250,000, a contracting officer will have more decision-making authority which should lead to faster acquisitions since decisions aren't being made by a committee. SAP does encourage competition, but only "to the maximum extent practicable," which means they may only require a few quick quotes instead of a lengthy RFP process.

One of the greatest benefits of SAP is less documentation for everyone involved. This equates to faster acquisitions that reduce the cost to the government by being more efficient.

What is a Micro Purchase?

A micro purchase is considered any purchase under the micro purchase threshold (MPT), currently at $10K for Federal entities. Non-federal entities can extend this up to 50K through a self-certification process under 2 CFR Part 200.320. Micro-purchases are also covered under SAP and can be references in FAR Subpart 13.2. But enough of the regulations.

If an acquisition is under $10K, it can be purchased using a government credit card (often referred to as a Government Purchase Card or GPC). In addition to contracting officers, thousands of other individuals in leadership positions are provided credit cards.

This method reduces paperwork even further by not requiring multiple quotes as long as the buyer feels that the price is reasonable. This is one of the rare situations where you could be on the phone with someone in the government and they could make a purchase from you over the phone without competition. Micro purchases are sole source.

Leveraging SAP

Ultimately, it's up to the CO or credit card holder to decide if they want to use this method or put a contract out via another method. You can help them make this decision by packaging your solutions UNDER the SAT or MPT.

Back to my friend William for a moment. How did he leverage SAP to win over $500K in government contracts? He spent roughly 30 months getting to know his prospects. He found out what their challenges were and built extensive relationships. Then and only then, he went back into his lab and created multiple micro-offers under $10K. Once he had these offers, he went back to his prospects and started pitching them. Some purchased right away and some took a few months. The exciting part of this is that once they've purchased from you, for example a micro purchase, they're more likely to pay $250,000 and then a $1M on the next contract.

While a CO can leverage SAP at any time, I've found that many love this method in Q4. In fact, one of my favorite strategies that I teach clients is to call all of their contacts in Q4 and ask if they have an unspent $50K training budget. Everyone has a training budget and they almost always have $50K in that budget that is going to go unused because they are focused on bigger things in Q4. Use this to your advantage. All the CO has to do is allocate that money to your company before the end of the fiscal year in order to count that as "spent." They like to do this because if they don't spend money in their budget, they risk losing it the next year.

Here's the great thing about training budgets. They are flexible. You can work with a CO to be creative with this money. This means it doesn't necessarily have to be used for training.

Chapter 24.
Introduction to Contract Vehicles

Do you need a vehicle? Maybe. Do you need every vehicle? Absolutely not!

Let's start out by talking about what a contract vehicle is and what it isn't. Vehicles are simply a mechanism that the government uses to streamline purchasing. Here's how they typically work. The government will put out an RFP and choose multiple "winners" of the RFP. Once they have the winners selected, the government will issue Task Orders (TOs) under the vehicle. These task orders, each requiring their own written proposals, turn into individual contracts under that vehicle.

The vehicle itself is the governing agreement between the government and the winners of the contract. These winners are often referred to as Primes. Depending on the size of the vehicle, the primes will often put together a team of companies. Sometimes they use a Joint Venture for this and sometimes it just requires standard teaming agreements for prime – subcontracting relationships.

The vehicle will usually have a spending limit or what is called a 'ceiling.' For example, my company, RSM Federal, is a subcontractor to a Prime on one of the VA's vehicles called VECTOR. It has a $5-billion-dollar ceiling. This means that over the life of the vehicle, the government can spend a max of $5 billion dollars.

Just because you "win" or you were awarded a vehicle doesn't mean you will win any of the Task Orders. In fact, just because the government awards a vehicle doesn't mean they will even issue any TOs. Having a vehicle is often referred to as "a license to hunt." Having a fishing license doesn't guarantee that you will ever catch a fish.

The real work begins once you are awarded the vehicle.

The most common terms you will hear around contract vehicles are IDIQs (Indefinite Delivery Indefinite Quantity), MATOCs (Multiple Award Task Order Contracts), GWACs (Government Wide Acquisition Contracts), and BPAs (Blanket Purchase Agreements – which aren't true contracts but agreements). These are all forms of vehicles. They have slight nuances. One of the main things that they all have in common is that they are typically awarded to multiple companies.

There is something called a SATOC (Single Award Task Order Contract). The difference between the first group of vehicles and a SATOC is that the SATOC will only be awarded to one company. The government will still use Task Orders as needed, but only one company will receive those.

A GSA Multiple Award Schedule (MAS) is also a vehicle. To get a GSA Schedule, you have to put together a proposal, have it reviewed by a Contracting Officer, negotiate pricing, and be awarded the schedule.

Most Common Questions About Vehicles

Do I need a GSA Schedule? The short answer is maybe. The best way to know if you need a schedule is to do your research. Depending on your target agencies and what you sell, you may not need one. At a minimum, you may not need it to get started in the government market. There's plenty of data to help you make this decision. If someone pressures you about a GSA Schedule, ask them to show you the data. *What percentage of purchasing for your products or services is flowing through GSA for your top agencies*? You need to know this before paying a dime toward GSA Schedule services.

How do you get on a vehicle? There are two main vehicle categories. There are open ones and closed ones. A GSA Schedule is an open one. You can apply for your schedule anytime. VA VECTOR is a closed vehicle. It was awarded a few years ago. The companies that won are the only companies that can bid on task orders until it comes up for recompete.

If the vehicle you want to pursue is open or on-ramping, all you have to do is get the proper paperwork (usually in the form of an RFP), fill it out (write a proposal) and submit it. The program office for that vehicle will review your submission and as long as you follow the instructions and meet the requirements, you will be awarded the vehicle. There may or may not be negotiations.

If the vehicle is closed, you either have to wait until the recompete rolls around OR you have to convince a current prime to add you to their team. This isn't easy unless you possess some unique skills.

What's the best vehicle for my agencies? Some of the best vehicles aren't the big competitive ones. Instead, they are small ones that are agency or even sub-agency specific. Some of those vehicles might be $5M or less and likely not have a lot of competition.

My recommendation comes back to research. Once we figure out WHO buys what you sell, the next step is figuring out HOW they buy. You are going to pull data from three main sources: SAM.gov's Data Bank, GSA's eLibrary, and the GSA Sales Query tool. These sources will tell you how your agencies are buying.

The other thing you need to do is talk to your target agencies. What vehicles do they prefer? What vehicles are they considering using over the next 12 to 24 months? What vehicles are they talking about on their website and social media? *Talk to your government prospects* and you will find out quickly which vehicles they like and which ones they don't.

What are the eligibility requirements for a vehicle? It depends on the vehicle. Some are based on socio-economic status. Some have other restrictions or requirements. All of this information will be on the vehicle's website or in the RFP.

Can I lose my vehicle? The short answer is yes. Each vehicle is a little different. You simply need to review your agreement. GSA is the most obvious one on this list. There are annual contract limits that you must meet in order to keep your GSA schedule. That number is currently $25K in sales per year. If you don't meet that number for three consecutive years, you will get a letter from GSA that basically says they are going to take your schedule away from you. You can appeal this twice. However, you must provide some level of assurance that you are working to correct this.

Other vehicles have different requirements. In most cases, you aren't going to lose your vehicle if you don't win task orders. However, I have seen agencies reach out to companies and ask them if they plan on responding to task orders if they go a long period of time without responding to anything. Inactivity or poor performance can cause your company to be removed from a vehicle.

What happens to the vehicle if I sell my company? There are many nuances to this, but in general, if the company is simply coming under new individual ownership, the vehicles will stay with the company unless the new owner doesn't qualify for some reason. For example, if the new owner doesn't qualify for 8(a), the company will lose their 8(a) status and lose vehicles that require that status. If the vehicle is NOT tied to a set-aside or some other requirement the new owner will keep the vehicle.

Task Orders

Task orders on a contract vehicle are very similar to a regular RFP with two key differences. The first is that the only people that will get the RFP notice are the companies that are on the contract vehicle. If the vehicle is GSA, the only companies that will see the RFP or RFQ are the companies with that particular special item number (SIN).

The second key difference is usually the turnaround time. Depending on the product or service, the proposal response will likely be significantly shorter and thus have a shorter deadline. The reason for this is that the companies on the vehicle have already submitted full proposals with extensive detail.

Remember, just because you are awarded a vehicle, doesn't mean you will be given task orders. You have to compete for them unless the vehicle is a SATOC. It helps that the competition pool is smaller on vehicles, but there's still competition and you have to respond to task orders. You can't win if you don't respond.

Tips for Winning Task Orders

Understand the vehicle: This should go without saying, but I'm going to say it anyway. This goes back to how many companies collect vehicles like baseball cards. I talk to companies all the time that have no idea why they are on a vehicle or what is even being purchased on the vehicle.

Understand the scope, limitations, and requirements of the vehicle. This allows you to position the use of the vehicle with your prospects and to talk intelligently about the vehicle with contracting officers and teaming partners.

Build relationships: Get to know the program managers and contracting officers for your vehicle. Attend their industry days and events and set up capability briefings. These people need to get to know you and your company.

Competitor research: Once a vehicle is awarded, it will become public knowledge who the other awardees are. Identify your top competitors and understand their strengths, weaknesses, and pricing. This is critical when it comes to determining what you are going to bid on, what you are going to pass on, and which RFPs will require teaming. However, few companies bring on additional teaming partners after the contract for the vehicle is awarded. Thus, you're researching the other companies on the Prime's team as well.

It's very easy to pull a competitor report in USASpending or SAM.gov. You can have this report in your hands in under 10 minutes in most cases. There's no excuse not to pull and review this data.

Don't bid on everything: Depending on the vehicle, you may be inundated with dozens or even hundreds of opportunities to bid every week. You need to be strategic about what you bid on. Just because you are on a vehicle *doesn't mean you should chase every task order*. Use your bid / no bid process to weed out the distractions.

If you believe that you are going to no bid a lot of task orders, let the contracting officer know that. This is part of building a strong relationship. Let them know that you are laser focused on the task orders in your wheelhouse. This is a simple way of keeping the lines of communication open.

I should also point out that some vehicles require a minimum number of responses to task orders. For example, one of my clients just received notification that they were selected as one of five Primes to win the contract. The notification reminded them that they are required to submit bids / proposals on at least 40% of the task orders in a twelve-month period. Again, this is why a strong bid – no bid process is important.

List of Popular Vehicles

Please note that all of these contracts have a shelf life. Depending on when you are reading this chapter, the vehicle might be in its next generation or even replaced by a contract with a new name.

You will notice that the vehicles I list below are predominantly for technology and professional services. GSA Schedules cover every industry. The ones below are the most widely recognized ones. There are hundreds of other vehicles. Many are agency or command specific. This is why researching your target agencies is so important.

8(a) STARS III: This contract is set-aside for 8(a) companies and focuses on IT services and custom IT services-based solutions.

Army ITES-3S: This vehicle is managed by the Army's Program Executive Office of Enterprise Information Systems (PEO EIS) under the Computer Hardware, Enterprise Software Solutions (CHESS) program. The focus is a wide range of IT services.

DHS PACTS II and III: PACTS III is set to replace PACTS II in 2024. The focus of this contract is non-IT services. It will include program management, administration, clerical, and technical services. This will be a 15-year contract.

GSA ASTRO: This is a broad series of contract vehicles that focuses on manned, unmanned, or optionally manned platforms and robotics for the Department of Defense.

GSA Multiple Award Schedule (MAS): This is commonly referred to as a GSA Schedule. The MAS consolidation of schedules happened in 2019. Now, contractors apply for a "schedule" under MAS based on their SIN (Special Item Number). Your MAS will be awarded based on your SIN.

HCaTS: The Human Capital and Training Solutions program is managed by the U.S. Office of Personnel Management (OPM). This contract is designed to help federal agencies hire and train personnel.

NASA SEWP: This vehicle is managed by NASA for acquiring a wide range of IT products (Hardware, software, and related services. As a write this, a draft RFP of NASA SEWP VI is on the street. Under the current RFP, the scope will be significantly expanded on the services side.

Navy Seaport-e: This vehicle is used for Naval commands to purchase professional support services and is managed by Naval Sea Systems Command (NAVSEA). The services include engineering, software engineering, configuration management, quality assurance, interoperability test and evaluation, logistics support, program support, and much more.

NIH CIO-SP4: This vehicle is administered by the National Institutes of Health (NIH) to allow federal agencies to purchase IT services and solutions. The primary task areas include IT services for biomedical research, CIO support, Imaging, Outsourcing, IT operations and maintenance, and several other IT related services.

OASIS+: As I write this, OASIS+ is in RFP review. Submissions for this vehicle happened in October of 2023. This vehicle will replace the original OASIS contract. The focus of this vehicle is to help federal agencies with the acquisition of complex professional services. Some of the services covered under this vehicle are: program management, management consulting, scientific services, engineering services, financial management, and logistics services.

Polaris: The primary focus of this vehicle is providing federal agencies with customized IT services and IT service-based solutions. Some of the services include data processing, hosting, computer programming, computer systems design and facilities management.

VA VECTOR: This is a professional services contract managed by the VA. This is an SDVOSB contract that provides administrative management and general management consulting services.

VETS 2: This is an SDVOSB contract vehicle. It provides a wide range of IT and IT service-based solutions. This vehicle is only for federal agencies.

Chapter 25.
Preparing to Kick Off a New Contract

Once the excitement dwindles down from winning a government contract, panic often sets in. You've won a contract, but have no idea what to do next. How do you prepare to kick off your new contract to make sure you can actually deliver on the promises you made? That's what I will cover in this chapter.

My goal for this chapter is to help you develop a kickoff checklist that you can use anytime you start a new contract. Since every company is different, what I expect is that you will review each section of this chapter and pull the relevant parts to develop your checklist.

There are two primary buckets that I put kickoff tasks into. Just about everything you can think of to kick off a contract will fall into one of these buckets. Remember, this is to setup your kickoff of a new contract. These two buckets are contract review and project planning.

Contract Review

Statement of Work Review: The first thing that I recommend you do is review the statement of work and contract terms. Contracts are often competed over several months. Don't expect to remember all of the details of any contract. Refresh your team on the requirements and the promises your company made.

During your review, make a list of all points of contact (POCs). All the points of contact! I don't care if it's a janitorial contract and you've got 16 different people that are going to be cleaning a building. You need to make a list of everybody that's going to be involved in this project, what their job responsibility is, who their supervisors are, who the project managers are, who your suppliers and subcontractors are, and any other relevant contact information. At a minimum, you need to capture: name, email address, phone number, position, and responsibility. This is your contract roster.

If there is a bank involved because you have a credit line or loan against the contract, be sure and add those people to your contact roster. Do this for anyone that touches this contract in any way.

Check the contract for compliance issues. If the contract is Service Contract Act (SCA) for example, are you following the guidelines of SCA with your employees both in the way you compensate them and your documentation? If not, you need to get this corrected ASAP. Do you have a solid plan for meeting the limitations on subcontracting (if you are using subcontractors)? Are you aware of all the FAR clauses in the contract and what they mean? If not, you need to stop and review any possible implications.

Compare your initial proposal requirements matrix to the contract. Has anything changed internally that might impact your ability to perform the work?

Simplify the SOW: The next thing that I recommend you do is simplify the statement of work for your team so that they understand it. Not everyone on your team may be technical in the areas that you are serving the customer. Consider your billing and HR teams. They likely don't know how to do the work, but they need to understand what work is being done and the type of people that need to be hired in order to do their job effectively. They need to set up internal codes to properly charge employee's time and invoice customers.

Don't toss out the statement of work. You're simply making it clear to the team what you've agreed to. Spell out the nuances. For example, if this contract calls for an adjustment to how you submit invoices, this is something that the billing team needs to know in this meeting.

Another challenge that comes up on a new contract is the systems, software and processes that you will be using. These are the types of things you should be communicating in this meeting. For example, if your team usually uses Dropbox for file sharing, but this contract requires using SharePoint, this internal process change needs to be brought up in your kickoff meeting.

Project Planning

Internal and Teaming Partner Kickoff Meetings: Next up on your list is your kickoff meetings. You need to facilitate a meeting with all key personnel that will be involved with the contract. I recommend you do this internally first and then externally with your teaming partners. I'm not saying repeat the entire meeting. If I just won a contract, I would sit down internally with my team, go through all the basics of the contract and then prep the team on our teaming partner(s). After this session, I have a similar call with my teaming partner(s).

I can't stress how important it is to have your internal kickoff meeting *first*. This allows you to discuss things that shouldn't be discussed on the partner kickoff call such as the politics of the situation, other teaming partner relationships, agency strategy, process review, and sensitive topics.

Review Challenges: Given the long lifecycle of a contract, you may have bid on a contract six months ago and pricing has changed significantly due to a random world event such as COVID. Maybe you bid with ten specific FTE resumes and four of those people are no longer with the company. Let's say this is a construction project. Maybe the contract requires a backhoe and yours caught on fire last week and is out of commission waiting on parts. There are all kinds of things like this that can happen between you submitting an RFP and winning it.

The problem with all of this is that most of this is considered, "your problem" as far as the government is concerned. Especially if you sign the contract. Which brings me to a very important side note. Before you sign a contract, make sure you don't have any significant changes that need to be addressed with the contracting officer.

Back to the COVID example, if you submitted a proposal before COVID that was awarded after COVID, you likely ran into several issues with pricing and availability of products and people. A lot can change in your world in as little as 30-days. Be sure and review what you are agreeing to before signing a contract no matter how exciting it is to get the award.

Client Kickoff Meeting: If necessary, have a kickoff call with the client. I say IF necessary because I've seen situations with products, where a kickoff isn't necessary. If it's a service's contract, you almost always have a kickoff call with the client. A client of ours recently won a small contract for $8,500 worth of power strips. This didn't require a formal kickoff meeting. However, if you have a kickoff meeting for something like this, it's likely going to take minutes and simply be for clarification purposes such as delivery address, time frame, invoicing procedures, etc.

Complex contracts definitely require a kickoff meeting. Why should you be the one to schedule this instead of the customer? You don't get paid until you deliver on a contract. It's easy for a contracting officer to award a contract and move on to the next item on their list. YOU need to be proactive to schedule this meeting. You might get some pushback. Especially if it's the end of the fiscal year. That's okay. Be polite and persistent. Your clients will thank you for being organized and on top of things.

Your client kickoff meeting should cover seven primary topics.

1. Introductions to your team and the customer
2. An overview of the statement of work
3. A review of deadlines and deliverables
4. Reporting and metrics
5. Invoicing
6. Q&A
7. Next steps

Chapter 26.
Mentor Protege

There are two primary mentor protégé programs (MPP): the SBA and the DoD MPPs. In addition to these two MPPs, there are several others. For example: DOE, FAA, and DHS. More agencies are looking at starting their own. The rules and benefits are slightly different for each program. Here is a list of the general rules for eligibility.

Protege Eligibility

- Must qualify as a small business for their primary industry
- Be a for-profit company or a small agricultural cooperative
- At least 51% owned and controlled by a U.S. Citizen or resident
- Able to demonstrate potential for success without the mentor
- Key personnel must have good character and a sound financial background
- The protégé must agree not to exceed the size standard for its primary industry during the MPP
- *Limited to two mentors during the company's lifetime*
- The MP relationship cannot exceed six years
- Have a proposed mentor

Mentor Eligibility

- Must be in good financial health and demonstrate a history of sound business practices
- The mentor must be approved by the agency or command to participate in the MPP
- Be able to carry out its responsibilities to assist the protégé
- Not appear on the federal list of suspended or debarred contractors
- Be willing to mentor and guide the protégé
- Limited to three protégés at any given time

My Advice

Don't jump into this.

This is a serious step for your business and like everything else in government contracting, it's not a silver bullet. In fact, many mentor protégé relationships slowly crash and burn over time. The reason is that they jump into the relationship to check a box. Don't do that. This is a serious step for your business and your company is limited to just TWO of these for the life of your company.

Before you get married, you should date. Picture this, you are in your favorite Taco Bell eating your Doritos locos tacos when in walks the best-looking person you've ever seen. You put down your taco, wipe that hot sauce off your face, and make your move: "Hi, my name is Mike. Want to get married this afternoon? I'll share my tacos."

As surprising as it may sound, that isn't good relationship advice. What you should do is date a bit before even thinking of getting married. But sadly enough, this is exactly how a lot of people approach the mentor protégé program. They want to jump into an MPP before they know anything about the mentor. All they see are dollar signs. Not smart business.

My advice is to slow down and focus on teaming with your potential mentor. It's okay if you go into the relationship with the goal of forming an MP, but it shouldn't be where you start. I suggest focusing on winning at least one, but preferably three contracts together. These contracts could be a mix of your company as the sub or prime. The point is not who the prime is. The point is to work and make money together.

You learn a lot from teaming with a company. The first thing you learn is whether you even like the company. What if the initial person you met was just a charismatic sales person and the manager you have to deal with is an ass? Do you want to be tied to this person for up to six years? Probably not. What if they have a bunch of dirty laundry, with a bad reputation, and you only uncover this once the MPP is approved and you start talking to prospects? Now you are tied to them. You have to dig deeper than surface level to get to know a company.

There are other benefits to teaming. The first is cash flow. As my partner Josh Frank would say, "it's not about the money, it's about the money." Talk is cheap. Revenue makes the world go around. Win a contract together or ask to be brought on as a sub to an existing contract. Get some money flowing to help add excitement to the relationship.

Does your mentor actually mentor you? You don't have to wait until you're under an official MPP to get mentorship. In fact, a great mentor will provide guidance every time you interact with them.

Does your mentor pay on time? It's about the money! Getting paid can be an issue. While your contracts always have terms, a lot of companies ignore them. Payment may be due in 30 days, but some companies are what we tend to label "slow pays" where they are closer to 35 or 38 days. I've even seen situations where a company is over 60 days late on their payment cycles. If this is a regular thing and your mentor can't fix this issue, that's a problem. If they always have an excuse for why they are late, that's a problem.

The government typically pays the prime within 30 days. It can then take several weeks or even a month for the prime to pay their subs. You need to take this into account if you're a subcontractor.

Is your mentor truthful with you? Clients regularly bring up mentor issues with me. One of the most common is that the actual customer let something slip in a meeting that didn't line up with what their mentor had been telling them. I have multiple examples that I could list where a mentor told one of my clients that the customer hadn't paid them and that's why they hadn't paid an invoice. When the client checked with the customer, the customer assured them they had paid the prime and even told them the date it was paid. The mentor was lying. Don't get into an MPP with a liar.

My last piece of advice is to sit down and work through the basics of a plan before going through the MPP process. Your MPP plan should answer the following questions:

- ☐ What are your goals?
- ☐ What are your milestones and timelines?
- ☐ What agencies are you going to target?
- ☐ How are you going to work together?
- ☐ What will be your call cadence (weekly, monthly)?
- ☐ What's the process for identifying and qualifying opportunities?
- ☐ What are your responsibilities as the protégé?
- ☐ What are their responsibilities as the mentor?
- ☐ Do you plan to form a joint venture?
- ☐ What metrics will you use to determine success?

What to Look for in a Mentor?

- ✓ They have experience and expertise in your industry
- ✓ They have a great reputation in the industry
- ✓ They have a great network and openly introduce you
- ✓ They have resources (people, systems, money)
- ✓ They provide training opportunities.
- ✓ They are seeking a long-term relationship beyond the MPP
- ✓ They are team players that will invite you to team
- ✓ They aren't solely dependent on your status
- ✓ You enjoy working with them
- ✓ They will actually MENTOR you!

Chapter 27.
Key Hires Along the Way

During your journey as a government contractor, you are going to hire a lot of people. The top four positions on my list are probably going to be your first hires. The order is going to vary from company to company. After that, it really depends on your needs. These are all positions that you will likely need along your journey. One way to rank these is by looking at two factors. 1) Which positions are going to drive revenue, and 2) Which positions will free up your time to do other things.

Key Positions and Descriptions

Business Developer (BD): This role is your sales person, but not just any sales person. I consider BD folks sophisticated sales people that can do basic research to find contact names and contract information, perform outbound sales activities, write or assist with basic quotes or proposals, manage relationships, and serve as a liaison between customers and your company.

Proposal Writer: First off, I typically don't recommend outsourcing this. It depends on your niche, needs, and the writer. I typically recommend hiring this person internally. This person is not a proposal manager. They are just a writer. Companies often hire this person before hiring a proposal manager. In this case, your proposal writer is the de facto proposal manager until they have the experience to serve as the proposal manager or until you can afford to hire a proposal manager. It just depends on the type of help you need.

Proposal Manager: The reason I put this role below the writing role is cash flow. You might not be able to hire a proposal manager initially, but you may need a writer to help you craft a proposal.

Proposal managers are often juggling multiple proposals and possibly multiple writers. Their job is to ensure that you are putting out a complete and *compliant* proposal that gives you the best chance of winning. They manage the process from A to Z and have the skills to pitch in where needed. They also cost more than the writer.

Assistant: Depending on your skillset, this might be the first person you hire. For example, if you are awesome at sales, but struggle with enough time to make calls, an assistant might be exactly what you need to free up some time.

Assistants come in all forms. Virtual, in-person, executive, and personal versus business, to name a few. You need to assess where you need help and then focus on dealing with those issues first. For example, when my children were young, we regularly had what I would call a nanny. She was an assistant. Her services ran us around $1K per month. She took the kids to school, picked them up, helped get them dinner after school, and watched them during meetings or when we went out of town for work. This freed up my wife and I to work in the business.

Capture Manager: I tend to not like this title, but it's common so I wanted to talk about it. You will often see capture managers in larger companies. They manage the "capture" of larger procurements. Their purpose is to laser focus their efforts (similar to a project manager) around a specific opportunity. Yes, they can often juggle more than one of these at a time, but they aren't doing daily prospecting like a business developer would.

Why would you want to hire a capture manager? A good example of this would be a multi-billion-dollar IDIQ. These types of opportunities often take months of work, strategy, team building, competitive pricing analysis, and much more. You want someone focused on this. However, I've seen companies hire capture managers for $5M opportunities. It just depends on your company's culture and requirements.

Project and Program Managers: As your business grows, you can't manage everything. You need people on your team to do this for you. One of my favorite positions to hire is a project manager. Depending on the complexity of the project, your PMs should be able to manage multiple projects at a time freeing you up to grow the business.

A great way to hire a program manager is to use the DoD SkillBridge Program. Many of my clients have utilized this program to hire multiple PMs. This is a DoD funded program that pays for service members to participate in the program. In fact, *you don't pay these folks*. They are still on active duty preparing for transition. Working with your company serves as an internship that gives them job experience for their resume and preps them for transition.

At the end of the term, you can hire them or get another intern from the SkillBridge program.

One of my friends, Eric "Doc" Wright runs a company called Vets2PM. His company is a SkillBridge host. His company can assist you in finding a PM intern.

Finance Person: Do you need an account, CFO, controller, etc.? It depends on your business. You need someone on your team that can help with compliance; making sure your books are in order; handle payroll issues; help with pricing; and anything else financial. Initially, a CPA might be all you need. It helps if this person understands government contracts. Otherwise, they are going to have a steep learning curve. I can tell you from experience, finance people don't tend to like learning new things or think outside of their little box. If you hire someone without government experience, they may struggle with government processes and procedures if they aren't open to learning new things.

Marketing Manager: As you grow, you are going to want someone on your team that is focused on your marketing strategy. This person should handle all external communication and activity. Need a new website? This person should be leading that project. Attending a conference? This person should be focused on all the details of the conference. Want to spin up social media? This person is going to manage this process and the social media team. Rebranding your company? This person is going to handle the messaging as well as the look and feel associated with the rebrand.

Techie's: When you are just starting out, there are all sorts of tech related people that you are going to hire. Web designers, engineers, app developers, software engineers, database analysts, cybersecurity experts, and systems engineers are just a few of the employees you might need.

Chapter 28.
Conferences

There are hundreds of government conferences. The challenge is not so much finding a "good one," but finding the right ones for your business and properly preparing for them. This chapter will give you some advice on how to prepare as well as provide you with a list of some of the top conferences for government contractors.

How do you find conferences to attend? Start with my list below. Ask contracting officers, small business reps, LinkedIn, and colleagues. Google it! A common search that I perform is "Government Conference (insert industry) (insert agency)." These are all simple ways to identify possible conferences.

 We have detailed strategies to help you evaluate which conferences are a good fit for your business. These documents can be found in Federal Access.

Do your homework on the conference. The conference website should have all the information you need: cost to attend; where it's located; how many people are expected to attend; daily agenda; speaker list; if they have a hotel block; airport information, etc. While doing your research, you should be able to see the session list on the agenda. Are your potential partners or clients speaking? If so, those are sessions that you probably want to attend.

Should you buy a booth? I recommend attending before setting up a booth. In fact, unless you are already conference savvy, you should attend at least three conferences before setting up a booth. You will learn a lot about what works and what doesn't by simply walking around and observing others. Exhibiting can be expensive. You can save a lot of time and money by educating yourself before buying your first booth.

Reach out to someone on the committee. You can do this before or after registration. If you have questions about the conference, don't be afraid to ask the team running the conference. If the website doesn't have information you need to make an informed decision, ask! Once you are registered, I suggest reaching out to someone on their board or staff (usually a program or executive director) and letting them know this is your first time attending and would like some advice or an introduction. Here's a little secret. These events are someone's baby. You need to find that person and connect with them. It's their job to make sure their conference is successful and people keep registering. It's in their best interest to help you by answering questions and making connections.

Register early! You can often save money on registration fees by getting the early bird special. If you've made the decision to attend, buy your tickets and book your hotel room. Hotel blocks tend to fill up quickly.

Side note: While I often stay at the conference venue for convenience, I may opt for another hotel or even an Airbnb instead. It depends on the cost. For example, I attended the regional 8(a) conference in Alaska in 2022. The hotel blocks filled up almost immediately and I missed the hotel block. The standard rate for rooms was $597 per night. Yes, you read that correctly. I was able to find an Airbnb for $600 for the entire week!

Setting goals for the conference. Your number one goal is to meet people, not sign a contract. You want to meet potential clients, teaming partners, small business reps, and the movers and shakers that support the conference. A great way to do this is by volunteering to help with setup. The conference team will almost certainly take you up on your offer to help with setup. You'll find that volunteering a couple hours at the event will often get you free registration.

Your secondary goal is to educate yourself. Government conferences are heavily focused on education tracks. Review the agenda and make sure you highlight all of the sessions you want to attend. You need to constantly work on being a better business owner and government contractor.

Map out your schedule: Once you know which sessions you are attending; I highly suggest blocking out time for meetings during the day. Plan for three to four blocks of time during the day where you can expand on conversations. Here's a great example of what that could look like. If you know you are attending sessions at 9, 11, 1, and 2, you could setup a block of time at 10 and 3 to connect with people you meet while socializing. Don't book more than 15 minutes with each person. Other attendees are busy and want to network and attend sessions as well.

Leave your evenings open to socialize. Every conference I attend has some sort of scheduled networking in the evening. Some of these events are on-site and some are just down the street. The purpose of these events is for you to network with other attendees. Food and drinks are often provided.

There are also private events. Sometimes, these conflict with conference events, but they might be more beneficial. For example, some of the big companies will have a client appreciation dinner or other event. They usually promote this at their booths. Depending on the event, you might consider attending this instead of a conference event.

While I recommend socializing, I do want to make a point that you shouldn't drink excessively at these events. You shouldn't do that regardless, but life happens. I'm not judging you. I'm just saying that when you are at an event, *you are working*. You can have a couple of drinks, but limit yourself. Your focus is not drinking. While I have no problem with having fun, your focus is building your business.

Do your follow-ups every night. Don't wait until you get back in the office on Monday. Reach out via email and LinkedIn every single night. In fact, don't even wait until the evening. If you have some downtime during the conference, send a few emails and LinkedIn invites from your phone.

A simple email follow-up may look like this:

"Beth, it was great meeting you today. I always love meeting other folks from Louisiana! I hope you enjoy the conference. I'll follow-up with you next week about (brief description of what you talked about). Safe travels!"

I have prewritten notes like the one above in my note's app on my phone. This allows me to quickly copy, paste, and customize an email or LinkedIn invite during downtime.

Follow-up within one week. Follow-up is extremely important. That's why I listed it twice! In addition to your daily follow-ups, you need to get on top of your next-steps immediately. One of the difficult things about conferences is remembering all the people you talk to. As time goes by, you will forget what you talked about and they will likely forget you. Don't give them time to forget. Touch base right away when you get back to the office.

Wear comfortable shoes. It's hard to think when your feet are bleeding. If the conference you are attending is on my list below, it's likely going to be at a large venue. These venues are notorious for having hotel rooms far away from the conference. I appreciate this for many reasons, but it also means that you are likely going to be walking a couple of miles per day. My record is eight miles per day for one of the VA conferences that was hosted in Atlanta.

If you purchase a pair of shoes just for the conference, break them in before the conference. You can do this by wearing them around the house for a day or two prior to attending the conference.

You will likely see me in one of two pairs of shoes at a conference. I'll either be wearing my Air Jordan's or Gatsby Oxford's. Just pick something that will be easy to stand and walk in for eight to twelve hours a day.

Get some rest. Don't stay up in the bar until midnight when you have to be up at six the next morning. It doesn't matter what you're drinking. You are going to be exhausted if you run yourself ragged. Do your best to get back to your room at a decent hour each night. Remember, you may have to do follow-ups and regular work before crashing for the night. Give yourself extra time to make sure you are well-rested and ready to go the next day.

In addition to getting plenty of rest, I make time during the day to take a couple of breaks. Lunch is typically not a break. You will likely be attending group working lunches. You need some downtime. Make a point of going back to your room, taking your shoes off, and just sitting for twenty minutes. You need breaks to stay fresh.

Speak when possible. My final piece of advice is to watch for the open call for speakers. Every conference does something similar to this where they allow people to submit abstracts for speaking sessions. This is a great way to get you and your company in front of more people. In fact, it's one of the top strategies we've used to build our business for more than 20 years.

Another bonus for getting chosen to speak is that the conference will usually comp your ticket or reduce your fee. Most conferences will at least reduce the ticket by 50% or give you a free day pass on the day you are speaking.

Michael's Top Conference List

This is just a partial list of conferences. I've either attended these or heard good things about them from clients and colleagues. If there is a conference that you attend that missed my list, please email me and I'll make sure it gets added to a future edition.

Yes, my list is primarily geared toward federal contracting. The SLED market has its own set of conferences. If you are SLED focused, I highly suggest you perform your own conference search for the particular state(s) that you want to target.

My favorite conferences: I can't possibly attend every conference every year. I do my best to mix in a new conference from time to time, but the short list below are the core five conferences that my team and I attend regularly.

- National 8(a)
- National HUBZone
- NVSBC VETS
- SAME SBC
- National Veterans Small Business Engagement

Other great conferences:

- RES - Tribal conference
- Alaska Regional 8(a)
- NHOA – Native Hawaiian Organizations
- NCMA World Congress
- Navy Gold Coast
- VIB Network
- Government Procurement Conference
- AFCEA - Multiple conferences throughout the year
- SOF Week
- AWS Public Sector Summit
- FedRAMP Annual Training
- RSA Conference
- NDIA
- Geospatial World Forum
- DoDIIS Worldwide Conference
- FOSE
- GEOINT Symposium
- TechNet
- NASCIO
- Professional Services Council (PSC) Annual conference
- Homeland Security Week

Chapter 29.
FAR References

Disclaimer: These regulations are updated regularly by the government. This list is here to bring awareness to these specific clauses. I highly recommend you Google them and read them for yourself.

This chapter is not designed to make you an expert on regulations or to expose you to everything. This was written for two purposes. 1. Almost every client of mine has asked me about popular regulations that pertain to their socio-economic status as well as what references they are likely to see in an RFP. This chapter is my shortlist of the most common regulations that I reference.

Let's start with a basic overview of three things:

What is the CFR? The Code of Federal Regulations is a compilation of rules published in the Federal Register by the executive departments and agencies. It's divided into 50 titles (major sections). Those titles include: General Provisions, The President, Domestic Security, Federal Elections, Banks and Banking, Food and Drugs, Highways, Labor, Internal Review, National Defense, Public Health, and much more.

What is the FAR? The Federal Acquisition Regulation is title 48 of the CFR. The FAR is the set of rules that govern the federal government's purchasing process.

What is DFARS? The Defense Federal Acquisition Regulation Supplement is a set of regulations that apply to all DoD contracts. It is a supplement to the FAR.

Key Sections

The following are parts and subparts of the CFR, FAR, and DFARS that you should be aware of. I suggest familiarizing yourself with each of them. You can Google them to learn more about each. This is just a basic introduction to key sections and what they cover.

13 CFR § 124: Covers the regulations and guidance related to the eligibility criteria and other requirements of the SBA's 8(a) small business development program.

13 CFR § 125.6: This is part of title 13 that focuses on business and assistance. 125.6 is specially about the small business subcontracting program. You can find information about a prime contractor's limitations on subcontracting in this section of the CFR.

20 CFR § 356.3: False Claims. The gist is that the government can come after you and/or your business if you provide false claims such as being a woman owned small business (WOSB) when you know you aren't a WOSB. This is not just limited to certifications. If you knowingly present false information to the government, you and/or your company could be fined, sued, and even debarred from doing business with the government.

FAR 4.12: This section covers Representations and Certifications (reps and certs). Reps and Certs are typically required to ensure compliance with various legal and regulatory requirements such as your small business status, socio-economic status, EEO, affirmative action, conflicts of interest, pricing, TIN verification, verification that a company has not been disbarred or suspended, as well as compliance with laws and regulations. This will likely be required as part of your proposal submission anytime you submit a proposal. You'll recognize many of these as part of your registration process in SAM.gov.

FAR Part 6.3: Other than full and open competition. This subpart provides guidance on the circumstances under which a contracting officer can use acquisition procedures outside of full and open competition. For example, the justification and approval process for sole-source awards.

FAR Part 13: Simplified Acquisition. This section provides guidance for simplified acquisition procedures (SAP) for contracts under $250,000.

FAR Part 15: This section of the FAR covers contracting by negotiation. It covers source selection, solicitation and receipt of proposals, contract pricing, award notifications, protests, unsolicited proposals, and more.

FAR Part 19: Covers all of the small business programs such as set-asides, size standards, the small business subcontracting program, contractor qualifications, and much more.

FAR Part 19.8: Covers 8(a) contracts.

FAR Part 22: Covers the application of labor laws for the purpose of government acquisitions.

FAR Part 44: Covers subcontracting policies and procedures

FAR Part 52.204-21: Covers the requirements for safeguarding covered contractor information systems.

FAR Part 52.219-14: Covers the limitations on subcontracting.

DFARS 252.204-7012: Covers the requirements for safeguarding covered defense information and cyber incident reporting.

Chapter 30.
The Marathon Mindset

Starting a government contracting business is a marathon, not a sprint. It takes time, hard work, and dedication to be successful. If you are physically fit, it takes an average of five to seven months to properly prepare to run a marathon. If you aren't in shape, it will likely take you a year or more…and that doesn't mean you are going win the marathon or even finish.

But Mike, what about all of those overnight successes that happen in government contracting? Overnight success often takes years of preparation. I've heard stories of people who have hit it out of the park in their first year in business. But, that's not the whole story. I know this for a fact because I've interviewed a lot of people who hit it big in their first year. All of them have one thing in common. They all prepared for months or even years before launching their business.

Go into this challenge with the understanding that this is a marathon and it's going to take time. That will help you in many ways. One is that you won't be too hard on yourself if you take longer to crush it than one of your colleagues. If you hit it big out of the gate, be thankful.

Before I open the can of worms about vision and goals, I want to address a common challenge - not letting your goals distract you from doing the work. You often won't know if your goals are even remotely realistic until you dive-in and start doing the work. This doesn't mean you change your goals; it means you might have to shift your deadlines.

I used to be really hard on myself for not hitting my goals. Then it occurred to me that goals are a simple math formula. Further, I've learned that success can be a habit. You can train yourself to make it automatic in your life and business, but you have to work to make it a habit. This often takes months of repetition of the right activities.

Good habits, like success, require being intentional about your goals, creating action steps, follow-through, and holding yourself accountable to the WORK!

My success formula: Hard work + Time = Success.

The only thing I can hold myself accountable to are the things to the left of the equal sign. Success is a product of hard work and time. Keep that in mind on our journey.

Vision and Goals

Your long-term vision. The first thing you need is a long-term vision. Tony Robbins says *the average person underestimates what they can achieve in five years, but overestimates what they can accomplish in a year*. This is human nature. We tend to be overly optimistic in short periods of time. I know a lot of people like this. They take on a big "weekend project" only to realize that it's going to take a month to pull it off.

One of my favorite proverbs is Proverbs 29:18: "Without a vision, the people perish." This holds true for every company. Without a vision to guide your company, the people (employees) will often just punch in and punch out. If you don't have a common goal to chase as a company, how can you possibly expect your team to achieve any meaningful results? You can't. And more importantly, you shouldn't hold them accountable for something that's a mystery to you.

What's your big vision?
What do you want to accomplish?
What's your big 10-year goal?

Theme for the year. I always have a theme for the year. My theme last year was "level up." My focus was leveling up areas of the business and my personal care. Having a simple theme helps me focus my energy and the rest of my goals.

My theme for this year is "Obsessed." I'm obsessed with *your* success. I want to focus all of my energy this year on finding new and innovative solutions to help my clients win more contracts, faster!

What's your theme for this upcoming year?

Year defining goals: I just recently started using this concept. I borrowed this from a talk I saw from Jesse Itzler. His thought was to have one year defining goal or event. I actually have five. I guess I'm an overachiever. :)

My year defining goals for this year:

1. To publish this book
2. A memorable family trip to Hawaii
3. See my daughter perform in the Macy's Thanksgiving parade
4. Lose 25 pounds
5. Increase our annual revenue by 25%

You may be wondering why I didn't put my revenue goal first. Well, it doesn't affect the other four goals. The other four goals can and should happen regardless of number five. I put these in the priority order that means the most to me.

You may also be wondering how these goals help with my theme. It's very simple to me. There's a lot of knowledge in this book. Not everyone can afford our coaching and training platform, but everyone can afford a book. My theme is being obsessed with your success. Our trip to Hawaii is a promise I made to my family five years ago. We agreed that once we were debt free, we would go to Hawaii as a family. Well, that happened and now it's time to fulfill a promise. That trip is going to fuel my soul for the year. My daughter's college color guard was chosen to perform at the Macy's Thanksgiving Parade. This is a once in a lifetime dream come true for her. Our family is going to celebrate this with her. Losing weight will make me healthier and more productive. Increasing revenue allows me to reinvest in the business and do some really cool things we have planned. My theme and those goals are intertwined.

Important Year One Goals: Outside of your long-term vision, theme, and year defining goals or events, I have a couple more that I recommend for your first year.

The first is setting a revenue goal. Be reasonable but push yourself. It's achievable to win $500K in your first year with the right effort.

Second, set a past performance goal. It is doable to win three to five small contracts in your first year.

Third, set a goal to meet all of the influential contracting officers for your top agencies. That number is smaller than you think. I bet there are less than 25 people that you need to meet at your agencies. Start by building an org chart of your target agencies. This will help you understand how the agency is structured and the silos in each agency.

Fourth, set a goal to build a relationship with four potential teaming partners for your teaming stable. That's just one per quarter.

These four goals are all you need for the foundation of your year-one business plan. You will want to break these down into activities (the 'hard work' piece of my success formula).

The Rule of 300

Your first year in business is likely to be intense. There's a lot of late nights and weekends. I have a simple rule that I suggest for everyone in their first year. It's called the rule of 300. You need to do ONE thing that moves the business forward six days a week for 50 weeks. That gives you one day off per week and two weeks of vacation that you don't have to think about the business.

I guarantee, if you do 300 things over the next year to build your business, you will have something significant to show for your effort. Make sure that six days a week, you are doing at least one thing that is going to help your business. It could be as simple as a phone call, email, or submitting a response to an RFI. It doesn't have to be earthshattering. When you stack up 300 little things together, you maintain momentum and create opportunities.

Continuous Learning

Don't treat your business like a side-hustle or job. Treat it like a passion. When you are passionate about something, you are constantly learning new things. When I look back at my journey over the last twenty plus years, one thing is very consistent. I constantly feel like I'm learning. Owning my business has been twenty years of learning. Sometimes the lessons are small and sometimes they are big, but I learn something on a weekly basis. Sometimes a daily basis.

My learning isn't accidental. When I don't know how to do something, I seek out a video, a book, a workshop, or a coach. There's no end to what you can learn about a topic. It doesn't matter what the topic is, you can always learn a nuance that makes you better. And that's the name of the game. Getting better!

I heard a quote from Jim Rohn about twenty years ago that has stuck with me. The quote is, *"Don't wish is was easier, wish you were better."* The concept is simple. If you get better, life gets easier.

Financial Stability

By now you should know this saying by heart, *"it's about the money."* You need to be brutally honest with yourself about money when you start a business. It doesn't matter if you started with nothing or a $100K small business loan. Breaking-even is priority number one. You can't afford to lose money for a year. The compounding effect financially and emotionally takes a toll on you. I know. I've been there.

Don't take a loan if you don't need it. Even then, do your best not to take one. Go get a part-time job before you take out a loan. You get quite a bit of motivation working for someone else. In my case, that was FedEx. It wasn't a fun job. I was being bossed around and yelled at by people half my age. It motivated me to make my business work so I could run my business full time.

When it comes to managing your finances, don't buy things you don't need. You don't need a new computer (yet). You don't need every fancy software program. You don't need the platinum level of support for your website. You aren't there. Grow into these things.

One of the biggest mistakes that people make besides large unnecessary purchases is unnecessary subscriptions. You don't need a paid subscription to everything under the sun. I'm still using the free version of HubSpot! We run a very profitable business and I'm not upgrading unless I absolutely have to. Are there essential subscriptions and memberships that will help run your business? Absolutely. But you don't need a subscription to everything just because your colleagues have them.

My last note about costs is about coaching programs. Yes, we are a coaching business. This may sound counterproductive for my business, but its honest. You don't need to be part of three mastermind groups, have a life coach, a business coach, and a wellness coach. If this describes you, you are likely addicted to coaching. This paragraph should serve as a mini-intervention for you. It hurts my soul when I see people spending 50K per year on coaching in a business that isn't even making 50K per year in revenue.

You likely need to be part of ONE coaching program. It could be a one-on-one program, a group coaching program, or a mastermind style program. You can accelerate your education and growth in the market by being part of the right program. I just want to encourage you to focus on one program at a time when you first launch your business.

I saw an interview with Denzel Washington while I was writing this chapter. He said, "Don't confuse movement for progress. You can run in place on a treadmill." This hit me hard. It's easy to see participation in a coaching group as movement and confuse it with progress. If you aren't taking action and that action isn't productive, you might be on a treadmill.

My last comment on financial stability is to focus on sales. Every. Single. Day! Back to my rule of 300. If you perform a sales activity every day, you won't be on a treadmill. You will be on your journey to success.

Adaptability

You don't know what you don't know. But there is one thing that I can almost guarantee, you will find out things on your journey that make you question yourself and your plan. Some of these lessons are just a distraction. Some of these lessons are a wakeup call that you are making a mistake and need to make a course correction.

The Marines have an unofficial slogan: Improvise, Adapt, and Overcome. This is the mindset you need as a business owner. In fact, it's not just as a business owner. If you are in sales, proposal management, or any other role in a company, one of your most valuable skills is adaptability.

Your job is to discern between distraction and valuable lesson and to implement the valuable lessons. For example, if I review your business plan and point out something that is obviously off-base, don't ignore me. One of the most common examples of this is with the key performance indicators (KPIs) for your sales and business development. Specifically, the number of RFPs you need to respond to. I reviewed three plans last week that severely underestimated the number of RFPs they need to respond to. Two of those companies took my advice. One said, "I guess we will see."

I recently reviewed a product plan for a client. It's a new physical product that is one-of-a-kind. They are a service company. We've already been down this road once this year. I'll reiterate, they are a service company. They don't understand product development or product sales. The first product they ran by me was something ridiculously outside their industry.

They are smart folks and have great ideas, but this was so wild that I begged them to shut down the idea. They did. Now they have another new shiny object. They don't want to give up the new shiny object because they've spent a lot of time and some cash investing in prototypes. While I love the idea, I cautioned them. They still have a long way to go. These other things are distractions. It's outside their core competency. If they don't hire a product manager, they are risking losing service sales by taking their eye off the ball.

You have to be able to spot things like this and adapt. In the example above, this company could make a ton of money on the product, but they are skimping on expertise in order to save money. In my opinion, they might as well put it on hold if they aren't going to go all in. Financially, they can't risk losing service sales and they aren't putting in the time, effort, or expertise that the product deserves.

Sometimes, it helps to be hardheaded, but you need to be open to advice and direction. Sometimes a simple tweak to your plan is all it needs to be smarter.

This reminds me of a simple story. When NASA was initially working on the space program, they determined that pens weren't going to write in space so they spent roughly $3 million dollars developing a pen that would write in space, upside down, under water, you name it. What did the Russians do? They used pencils. Sometimes we complicate things for no reason and our pride gets in the way of adapting.

Quality Performance

When it comes to the success of your brand, there's nothing more important than the quality of your performance. When I think of my favorite shoes, I go back to my first pair of Air Jordan's. The V and VIIs were my favorite. If you've never worn a pair of these, it's quite an experience. They were the softest pair of shoes I'd ever worn. Putting them on was literally like walking on a cloud. This will always be my favorite pair of shoes.

The shoes led me to the Air Jordan clothing line. My favorite t-shirts are Air Jordan. I'm very particular about the feel of clothing. I probably have some sort of texture disorder because I won't wear clothes unless they feel a certain way.

The other thing that I LOVE about the Air Jordan sub brand of Nike is that all of these products last forever. I wore those shoes forever. I would probably still have them if I hadn't left them at home when I joined the Army. Not sure what my mom did with them. I had my first shirt for over twenty years. Pretty sure a girlfriend stole my favorite one.

I have a favorable view of this brand because the quality and performance are outstanding. For me, no other brand has ever come close to the Air Jordan brand. I seek it out. In fact, I'm currently on the hunt for a pair of black Air Jordan V and VIIs. If you know where I can get a pair, please let me know. I'll give you a free coaching session if I end up finding a pair. That's how much I love this brand.

When it comes to your brand, DO NOT skimp on quality and performance. Make bold claims and then back them up by kicking ass!

Chapter 31.
Hiring a Coach

At this point in the book, you are either extremely confident that "you've got this" or you are completely overwhelmed. There's a lot to this business. This chapter isn't necessarily meant to be a sales pitch, but I am an advocate for having a coach and I want to give you my two cents on how coaching can help you, what to look for in a coach, and the fact that you can get a coach without breaking the bank. I'll also cover how we work with companies like yours. If we can work together, great. If not, that's fine. But I would suggest you find someone that can help you.

Three Benefits of Having a Coach

There are three particular things at the top of my list of benefits for having a coach. The first is that they aren't as close to your business as you are. They can see the forest through the trees. You are so close to your business that you often can't see what you are doing right or doing wrong. It's also hard for most business owners to be objective about their business. A great coach can provide this insight. They can spot things you can't see no matter how hard you look.

The second benefit is the amount of time they will save you. You can often get to your destination on your own, but you will go faster with a guide. I've been in this business for over twenty years. In that time, I've coached and worked with hundreds of business owners. I've sat in thousands of consultations. I've seen nearly every mistake you can make. I've listened to overly optimistic people tell me they were going to climb Mt. Everest and then never even buy the plane ticket to Nepal. My advice can shave off months or even years of frustration.

The third benefit of a great coach is a no bullshit approach. When it comes to my coaching, I believe that the hard-truth is more beneficial than just having a cheerleader encouraging stupid behavior. Is that blunt enough for you? Remember, I said no bullshit. If you are doing something stupid, you need to hear that. You also need to be called on your bullshit. A coach once told me that reasons are just excuses in fancy clothing. Life happens. We all have setbacks and roadblocks. But that can't be your life. You can't grow a business when you have a pile of excuses holding you back.

One of the reasons people don't follow the Marine motto of Improvise, Adapt, and Overcome is because they can't be honest with themselves about the things holding them back. One of my jobs as a coach is to help you overcome obstacles by spotting and confronting issues and challenges.

What to Look for in a Coach?

Specialization: I came from a business model that promoted working with generalist coaches. While that's helpful in certain situations, it's not applicable for government contractors. You need a coach that understands the market. I don't need to understand your business to help you. I need to understand the market you are trying to sell to.

I mentioned in the introduction of this book that I primarily work in the Federal market. That's my specialization. Everything I teach revolves around this market. Do I teach a lot of strategies that are market agnostic? Absolutely! But the nuances of my coaching are focused on Federal government contractors. These companies are going to get the biggest bang for their buck with me.

You need a coach that is going to focus on your target market. They will understand how to find your buyers, how to sell to them, and how to grow a business in that market. It helps if they know your industry. Our team is setup that way. We all know government contracting, but have industry and skill niches. If you need help in the medical field or with a GSA Schedule, I set you up with Rich Earnest. If you need help with systems, certifications, and your market strategy, you work with Ashley Duwel. If you are a disadvantaged business in the tech space and need help with business development, I'm going to set you up with David Neal. Specialization helps accelerate the process. We have a dozen coaches that specialize in bridging government sales strategies with business strategy.

Reputation: "You come highly recommended." Almost every conversation I have with a prospect starts out with them saying they know someone or multiple people that have recommended me or my company. I've reached this strange stage of my business where I've often never heard of the person recommending me. It's strange because I never dreamed that would happen. It's humbling and it motivates me to keep up the good work.

I've talked multiple times in this book about your brand and the quality of your products and services. Your reputation is a reflection of a job well done. It takes decades to build a reputation and one moment of carelessness, foolishness, or stupidity to destroy it. When you speak to someone who has a great reputation, you typically realize in the first five minutes why they have maintained it over the years. They are the real deal. That's what you want to look for in a coach.

Alignment of Values: I gave you a glimpse of my values in the introduction of this book. Those values serve as a filter for me to know when I shouldn't work with someone. They also serve as a filter for potential clients. If a potential client doesn't like two or three of my core values, they likely won't ever reach out to me. And I'm just fine with that. This eliminates potential conflict.

If you are interviewing a potential coach, business partner, employee, or anyone else that you intend to work with, it's important to know what their core values are. I would argue that it doesn't matter how small their role is in your business. Whether they are an executive or a janitor, everyone you associate with is a reflection of you and your business. Everyone on your collective team should be in close alignment with your values. Close means that they don't have to be 100% in alignment, but they also shouldn't be at the other end of the spectrum.

Chemistry: You can respect someone and not get along with them. This is a hard one to judge during a consult. However, you will either develop chemistry with your coach or you won't. This is something to watch for during your relationship.

A great sign of chemistry is when clients don't just talk about business. We talk about their personal life, hobbies, and other interests. This means we are becoming friends, not just business associates. There's nothing wrong with keeping your relationships 100% professional at all times. But if you want a deeper connection, getting personal helps. I always go there with clients. Even if it's subtle, I want to know what drives them. I use that to fuel our relationship in order to help them hit their goals. And I use it as a filter to guide them out of situations that don't align with their desires.

Contract: One of the biggest things for me is having an escape clause if either of us determine this isn't working. Both parties typically have the best of intentions, but sometimes things don't work out. Even if someone has a 12-month contract, there should be a termination clause. This allows you or the coach to gracefully exit the agreement.

Cost: It's about the money, right? Just because you want to work with Tony Robbins doesn't mean you can afford him. His one-on-one coaching clients pay him seven figures a year. That's out of reach for most people.

Cost shouldn't be the only factor when considering a coach, but it's a key consideration. For a moment, let's disregard the value you'll receive. What can you afford? Most coaches have multiple levels of coaching. You may not be able to initially start with their highest tier, but you can get started on an entry or mid-level program and grow from there.

If you start at a high tier that is technically out of your reach, you could get resentful with your coach very quickly if you don't achieve massive results in a short period of time. That doesn't mean the coach isn't providing massive value. It could mean your expectations are out of line or you haven't given the program enough time. These feelings tend to appear when the cost is just out of your reach and instead of choosing a plan that fits your budget, you stretch yourself beyond your means and that puts unnecessary pressure on you and your coach.

I've had clients on plans that were $10K a month and thought it was a steal for the value. I've had clients at $100 that complained because they wanted my first born and I wouldn't give it to them. It's all about perspective.

What I can tell you is that the goldilocks approach works. Choose a plan that you are comfortable with and that relieves a lot of stress from you and the coach. Then the focus can be on your objective: growing your business.

How we Work with Clients

RSM Federal has two primary methods of working with clients. We have a group model and a one-on-one model. Most people who are interested in the group model simply visit our website federalaccess.com and sign up for either a monthly or annual plan.

If you are interested in one-on-one coaching, you will likely call, email, or grab a time on our calendar. Josh and I have free consults that we do with clients to help them determine if there's a good fit for coaching and then we make recommendations. Those recommendations can range from $249 per month for group coaching to as much as $9,995 for one-on-one consulting. However, our average coaching client starts with FastTrack one-on-one coaching for $2,995 per month.

Once you are signed up as a client, there's a couple of paths that you can take. If you are group coaching client, you will get a welcome checklist and access to the Federal Access Vault of resources, our coaching and training platform with every template, tactic, and strategy you need to win contracts.

If you are a one-on-one coaching client, you will go through an intake process. That process is an onboarding form on our website that you fill out that asks several questions. It takes about 30 minutes to complete this form. Once you complete the intake form, we ask that you send us several documents for us to review. This includes your capability statement, corporate deck, any relevant marketing material, and a copy of your last three bids or proposals. We use all of this information as part of our market research for your kick-off call. The last step in your intake process is to schedule your kick-off call with your coach.

During your kick-off call, your coach will review all of their research and make several recommendations. This session is often like drinking from a firehose. We cover a lot of ground in a short period of time. This serves as the foundation for future coaching sessions.

After your kick-off call, clients typically start working on their strategy. We help you identify who buys what you sell, how they buy what you sell, and we start working on your processes. The reason I say typically is because every client is different. Some clients are new to the market and need a lot of education. Some clients have been in the market for 25 years, are making $250 million annually, but have plateaued. One-on-one coaching is customized to your company, the product or services you sell, where you are today, and specifically what you need.

Strategy development often takes a month or two. Sometimes three. Once we work through the nuances of your strategy, it's almost all about execution. At this phase of our coaching relationship, we move into more of a strategic advisor role helping you execute. You may need to be prepped for a capability briefing on your next call or you may need us to review an RFP with you. It depends on your needs and requirements.

My goal with every client is that you are building your pipeline within three months. It may take you six months to fill it, but I want you engaging prospects and lining up contracts as fast as possible. This is the best way to accelerate the process of winning your first contract. If you don't bid, you don't win.

A Small Favor

I want to thank you for investing your time and money with me.

If you enjoyed and gained value from this book, I would be *very **grateful*** if you would **post a five-star review on Amazon.** Even if you did not buy this book on Amazon, *you can still leave a review there*!

I'll even make you a deal. If you screenshot your review and email it to me at mlejeune@rsmfederal.com, I'll send you something special.

Your review provides immense value. It validates that my passion has provided you with value!

Thank you in advance!

Other RSM Federal Resources

Federal Access (FA)

The flagship solution of RSM Federal. Federal Access (FA) is our award winning and nationally-recognized coaching and training platform that helps companies win government contracts.

FA has more than 200 step-by-step strategy guides, over 100 templates, 150 training videos and webinars, WEEKLY live interactive Q&A calls, and the best Subject Matter Expert (SME) support for government contractors. You can start your journey with us today by visiting:

https://Federal-access.com/NewToGovConBook

Amazon #1 Bestselling Books

The Government Sales Manual
Visit https://www.amazon.com/dp/1733600981

Game Changers for Government Contractors
Visit https://www.amazon.com/dp/1733600949

An Insider's Guide to Winning Government Contracts
Visit https://www.amazon.com/dp/173360099X

Becoming a GovCon Expert
Visit https://www.amazon.com/dp/1733600965

Podcast

Game Changers for Government Contractors is the #1 podcast in the Nation for government contractors. Every week, we interview subject matter experts and provide game-changing strategies to help you win more government contracts. Game Changers is available on just about every podcasting app and YouTube. Simply search for Game Changers for Government Contractors.

https://bit.ly/GameChangersForGovernmentContractorsPodcast

Connect with Me on LinkedIn

If you gained value from the content and concepts in this book, I highly suggest that you and I connect on LinkedIn. Just send me a request. Be sure and mention that you read my book!

Here is the link to my profile: https://www.linkedin.com/in/michaeljlejeune/

About RSM Federal

The Art and Science of Government Sales™

RSM Federal is an award-winning coaching and consulting firm that has helped their clients win over $14.6 billion in government contracts, trained more than 23,000 contractors, and have written four Amazon #1 bestselling books on the subject of government contracting. Over 2,500 government contractors trust the Federal Access coaching and training platform as their primary source for GovCon education, coaching, training, and practical strategies for winning government contracts.

Providing the **Art and Science of Government Sales**™, RSM Federal has quickly become a nationally trusted educator, trainer, coach, and consultant to other companies, associations, and coalitions.

We emphasize basic and advanced strategies tailored specifically for your company to accelerate success and revenue. We leverage a proven combination of industry expertise and measurable strategies to deliver cost-effective and high-value results for our clients.

With nationally recognized and award-winning expertise and hundreds of resources, tactics, templates, and step-by-step strategies, your company can immediately accelerate your marketing, prospecting, sales, teaming, and proposal activities - literally overnight.

About Michael LeJeune

Author

MICHAEL LEJEUNE is a bestselling author and master coach with RSM Federal. He has over 20 years' experience working in the Federal market. Michael hosts the wildly popular podcast Game Changers for Government Contractors, manages the Federal Access Coaching and Training Platform, and specializes in helping government contractors' brand themselves as Subject Matter Experts in their niche.

Michael specializes in breakthrough executive coaching. He works primarily with companies that are either new to the market or have plateaued and don't know what to do next.

You have likely heard Michael on the nation's leading government contractor podcast - Game Changers for Government Contractors. Michael started this podcast in 2016. Thousands of contractors listen to Game Changers every month. Game Changers is available on every major podcasting app.

Michael served four years in the Army at Ft. Hood. First in the 2nd Armor Division and then with the 4th Infantry division from 1995 to 1999. Michael received numerous awards while working on the FORCE XXI program for the Army testing new equipment and technologies. This is how Michael was introduced to government contracting.

Michael started his corporate career in 1999 with General Dynamics in the highly competitive virtual collaboration space. His primary clients were the Department of Defense, Intelligence Agencies, and the Joint Forces Commands.

Michael currently resides in the small town (pop. 335) of Watauga, TN with his wife, two daughters, five dogs, and a cat that scares the hell out of all of them.

Acronyms

Here's a list of some of the most common acronyms that you are likely to come across as a government contractor.

ANC	Alaska Native Corporation
BAFO	Best and Final Offer
BIC	Best In Class
BOA	Basis of Award
BPA	Blanket Purchase Agreement
CCR	Central Contractor Registration (now part of SAM)
CFR	Code of Federal Regulations
CMMC	Cybersecurity Maturity Model Certification
CMMI	Capability Maturity Model Integration
CO or KO	Contracting Officer (DoD uses KO to distinguish from Commanding Officers
CONUS	Inside the continental United States
COTS	Commercial Off-The-Shelf
CPARS	Contractor Performance Assessment Review System
CUI	Controlled Unclassified Information
CTA	Contractor Teaming Arrangement
D&B	Dun & Bradstreet

DAR	Defense Acquisition Regulation
DFARS	Defense Federal Acquisition Regulations Supplement
DHS	Department of Homeland Security
DoD	Department of Defense
DoJ	Department of Justice
DoR	Dealer of Record
DoT	Department of Transportation
DUNS	Data Universal Numbering System (Replaced with SAM UEI)
EDWOSB	Economically Disadvantaged Woman-Owned Small Business
EEO	Equal Employment Opportunity
EPA	Economic Price Adjustment
EPLS	Excluded Parties List System (now part of SAM)
ERM	Electronic Records Management
EULA	End-User License Agreement
FAI	Federal Acquisition Institute
FAR	Federal Acquisition Regulation
FAS	Federal Acquisition Service
FBO	Federal Business Opportunities (also known as FedBizOpps) / Integrated into SAM.gov
FCA	False Claims Act
FOCI	Foreign Ownership, Control, or Influence
FOIA	Freedom of Information Act

FPDS	Federal Procurement Data System
FSC	Federal Supply Class
FSS	Federal Supply Schedule
FSSI	Federal Strategic Sourcing Initiative
FTA	Free Trade Agreement
FTE	Full Time Employee
FY	Fiscal Year
GAO	Government Accountability Office
GPA	Government Procurement Agreement
GPC	Government Purchase Card
GSA	General Services Administration
GWAC	Government Wide Acquisition Contract
HCaTS	Human Capital and Training Solutions
HHS	Department of Health and Human Services
HUBZone	Historically Underutilized Business Zone
IDIQ	Indefinite Delivery/Indefinite Quantity
IFF	Industrial Funding Fee
ISBEE	Indian Small Business Economic Enterprise
ISR	Individual Subcontracting Report
ITAR	International Traffic in Arms Regulations
LOS	Letter of Supply
MAC	Multiple Award Contract
MAP	Minimum Advertised Price

MAS	Multiple Award Schedule
MATOC	Multiple Award Task Order Contract
MBE	Minority Business Enterprise
MFC	Most Favored Customer
MOBIS	Mission Oriented Business Integrated Services
MOT	Maximum Order Threshold
MPT	Micro-Purchase Threshold
NAICS	North American Industrial Classification Standard
NDAA	National Defense Authorization Act
NGO	Non-governmental organization
NHO	Native Hawaiian Organization
OCONUS	Outside Continental United States
ODC	Other Direct Costs
OHA	Office of Hearings and Appeals
OIG	Office of Inspector General
OMB	Office of Management and Budget
ORCA	Online Representations and Certifications Application (now part of SAM)
OSBDU	Office of Small and Disadvantaged Business Utilization
OSBP	Office of Small Business Programs
PCO	Procurement Contracting Officer
PIV	Personal Identification Verification (Federal)
PO	Purchase Order

PPIRS	Past Performance Information Retrieval System
PRC	Price Reduction Clause
PSC	Product and Service Codes
PSS	Professional Services Schedule
PWS	Performance Work Statement
QAP	Quality Assurance Plan
RFI	Request for Information
RFP	Request for Proposal
RFQ	Request for Quote
SAM	System for Award Management
SAP	Simplified Acquisition Procedures
SAT	Simplified Acquisition Threshold
SATOC	Single Award Task Order Contract
SBA	Small Business Administration
SBDC	Small Business Development Center
SCA	Service Contract Act
SCLS	Service Contract Labor Standards
SDB	Small Disadvantaged Business
SDVOSB	Service-Disabled Veteran-Owned Small Business
SIC	Standard Industrial Classification
SIN	Special Item Number
SIP	Schedule Input Program
SOW	Statement of Work

SSQ	Schedule Sales Query
SSR	Summary Subcontracting Report
T&C	Terms and Conditions
TAA	Trade Agreements Act
TAPS	Temporary Administrative & Professional Staffing Services
TDR	Transactional Data Reporting
USC	United States Code
USDA	United States Department of Agriculture
VA	Department of Veterans Affairs
VOSB	Veteran-Owned Small-Business
WOSB	Woman-Owned Small Business
WTO	World Trade Organization

Made in the USA
Las Vegas, NV
06 November 2024